LAW
AND
CURRENT
WORLD ISSUES

LAW
AND
CURRENT
WORLD ISSUES

Columbia Law School Symposium 1986

The Role of Law and Lawyers in South Africa
Can Tort Law Handle Modern Industrial Accidents?
New Limitations On Defendants Right to Counsel
Terrorism and the Law

Edited by
NANCY WIGHT

OCEANA PUBLICATIONS, INC.
New York • London • Rome

Library of Congress Cataloging-in-Publication Data

Columbia Law School Symposium (27th : 1986)
   Law and current world issues.

   1. Criminal law—United States—Congresses.   2. Torts—
United States—Congresses.   3. Criminal law—Congresses.
4. Torts (International law)—Congresses.   5. Law—
South Africa—Congresses.   I. Wight, Nancy.   II. Columbia
University.   School of Law.   III. Title.
KF9219.A2C65   1986   345   87-12363
ISBN 0-379-20780-X   342.5

© Copyright 1987 by Oceana Publications, Inc.

All rights reserved. No part of this publication may be reproduced or transmitted in any form or by any means, electronic or mechanical, including photocopy, recording, xerography, or any information storage and retrieval system, without permission in writing from the publisher.

Manufactured in the United States of America

TABLE OF CONTENTS

INTRODUCTION / v
Phillip A. Lacovara
President, Columbia Law School Alumni Association

DEDICATION / vii

THE ROLE OF LAW AND LAWYERS IN SOUTH AFRICA / 1
Professor Jack Greenberg, Moderator

CAN TORT LAW HANDLE MODERN INDUSTRIAL ACCIDENTS? / 39
Professor Arthur W. Murphy, Moderator

NEW LIMITATIONS ON DEFENDANT'S RIGHT TO COUNSEL / 85
Professor Vivian O. Berger, Moderator

RECEPTION AND LUNCHEON REMARKS / 113
Hon. Rena K. Uviller, Presiding
Honoring Judge Benjamin Kaplan and Judge James D. Hopkins

TERRORISM AND THE LAW / 131
Sulzbacher Memorial Lecture
Hon. Abraham D. Sofaer
Introduction by Dean Barbara Aronstein Black

APPENDIX / 165
Symposium Program

INTRODUCTION

PHILIP A. LACOVARA
President, Columbia Law School
Alumni Association

In 1957 the Survey Committee of the Columbia Law School Alumni Association recommended the organization of an annual conference at the Law School to which all alumni would be invited. The programs adopted by the Survey Committee's recommendations have indeed proven their worth.

The twenty-seventh such event, now called the annual Columbia Law School Symposium, brought together on April 5, 1986, three outstanding panel discussions in addition to the thirteenth annual Sulzbacher Memorial Lecture. The topics were wide-ranging and included something for everyone. "The Role of Law and Lawyers in South Africa" was a thought-provoking discussion on human rights and the South African liberation movement. It was led by Professor Jack Greenberg and included Sonny Venkatrathnam, a South African, who had been a prisoner on Robben Island. The panel on tort law, moderated by Professor Arthur Murphy, was concerned with industrial accidents, and addressed itself broadly to the ability of the tort system to handle cases presenting multiple claims for bodily injuries and physical injury to property. Most agreed that mass tort (e.g., Agent Orange, asbestos, toxic torts) are the principal areas of difficulty, but predictably the system had its defenders as well as critics among the panelists and the audience. The panel on "New Limitations on Defendants' Right to Counsel," presided by

Professor Vivian O. Berger, also brought together academics as well as practitioners on a subject of extreme interest on which there was considerable disagreement, both among the panelists and in the audience. Matters such as the subpoenaing of lawyers and the forfeiture of fees provoked a lively discussion and a wide range of opinions emerged, expressed with considerable vigor.

"Terrorism and the Law," our afternoon lecture, was a timely topic of this worldwide issue, presented by the State Department's Legal Adviser, the Honorable Abraham D. Sofaer.

To bring this program to an even wider audience, we have transcribed these discussions from tapes and tried to keep the flavor of their spontaneity.

The Columbia Law School Alumni Association will be forever grateful to the late Walter Werner, who, as Adolf A. Berle Professor, served for three years as Faculty Chairman of the Symposium Committee. The triumphs of the 1986 Symposium are a lasting tribute to his prodigious efforts and keen sensitivity. We are also most appreciative of the work of the Honorable Rena K. Uviller '62, who lent her considerable skills in coordinating and presiding and, thereby, helped transform exciting ideas into a stimulating and enjoyable program.

December 1986

DEDICATION

WALTER WERNER
(1915-1986)

We dedicate *Law and Current World Issues,* the *Columbia Law School Symposium 1986,* to the memory of Walter Werner, Adolf A. Berle Professor Emeritus, Faculty Chairman of the Symposium Committee, for his tireless work on this most successful and stimulating program which took place at Columbia on April 5, 1986. His lively and creative intelligence determined the provocative range of the topics discussed and helped bring together outstanding participants. We are grateful, too, for the selfless spirit in which he undertook this and every other assignment at the Law School.

THE ROLE OF LAW AND LAWYERS IN SOUTH AFRICA

Moderator:
JACK GREENBERG
Professor of Law and Vice-Dean,
School of Law, Columbia University

Panelists:
LOUIS HENKIN
University Professor, Columbia University

SYDNEY KENTRIDGE
Senior Counsel, Johannesburg, South Africa
Attorney for the families of Steve Biko
and Winnie Mandela

SONNY VENKATRATHNAM
Former political prisoner
Member of the Unity Movement
Durban, South Africa

PROFESSOR GREENBERG: We will discuss the role of law and lawyers in South Africa, and I will introduce the three panelists. The first of our speakers is Sonny Venkatrathnam, who is a South African. In 1963 he was a teacher and engaged in opposition to what was then called Bantu education, the educational system for blacks. He was fired from his teaching job and banned. That means restrictions were placed on his movements, on the number of people he could meet, and where he could meet them. Venkatrathnam then decided that the better course of valor was to become a lawyer and began studying law. He could not repress his oppositional instincts, however, and was banned again, arrested, and unable to attend law school. He continued his wayward ways and in 1970 was arrested and detained. Finally, the authorities couldn't stand him any longer and sent him to Robben Island. Venkatrathnam was there for a period of approximately ten years, was released, and banned once more.

In order to make a living he opened a service station, which he ran for a number of years. Then he became a focal point of political opposition, particularly in the effort to introduce the tripartite constitution which is in South Africa today; one for whites, coloreds, and Indians, excluding the vast number of African blacks, as well as giving only very limited power to those groups that are newly included. His service station lease was canceled by the Mobil Company; he went out of business and decided that the best thing to do was to come to Columbia and get a master's degree in International Affairs where he is studying today. Venkatrathnam is also participating in and attending a seminar which is being taught by Professor Stephen Ellmann and Sydney and Felicia Kentridge.

Sydney Kentridge, I think, is, by common consent, the leading lawyer in South Africa. There he is referred to as an advocate; in England he would be called a barrister or queen's counsel; in South Africa he is senior counsel. He has an enormously successful career in what one might call conventional, corporate and business law, but unlike American lawyers with practices of this sort who rarely, if ever, handle a political or human rights case, or if they do, handle one or two in a lifetime, he has regularly been involved in litigation of such matters. In 1958-59, he was counsel in the famous treason trials in which Nelson Mandela was a defendant. He is probably best known in America for his representation of the Biko family in the inquest which first--I won't say first-- brought to American attention the great evils of the South African apartheid system, but certainly most forcefully brought it to American attention. Most recently he has been known as counsel to Winnie Mandela.

On my right is Louis Henkin, who is University Professor at Columbia. I hope he will not object to my calling him the great legal thinker and theoretician of human rights law in this country. One of the world's leading experts on international law, he is the reporter of the American Law Institute Restatement of International Law in the United States. He is a human rights scholar and human rights activist.

MR. VENKATRATHNAM: My duty today as a panelist is to introduce South Africa to you. I will try to sketch the development of the liberation movement in South Africa and pose, as sharply as I can, the changes in the judiciary or the response of the legal system. Perhaps Sydney Kentridge can take it from there. One of my main arguments would be that the apartheid system that exists in South Africa today is not something that descended upon South Africa or was thrust upon it since 1948. This is the myth that is passed around; it is a myth that is being put forth by both the international and the local South African press in South Africa. But, looking at the history and development of South Africa over the last 250 years, one would find very clear traces and examples of apartheid. One could go back to the early eighteenth century when a system of segregation was introduced by the settler regime at that particular time. True, it was not the sort of pass laws and reference books that the people have to carry today, but the seeds of apartheid were sown way back in 1797 when the slaves that were brought out from the East and from Africa were controlled in the movement and residential areas where they were forced to live.

At the same time there was an influx of white settler population in South Africa, and one found a lot of immigrants, settlers from Europe, who came because of the religious problems they were facing there. There was an upheaval--people were not happy with the change of social structures in Europe. One must remember that Europe too, at this time, was undergoing tremendous social change as a result of the Industrial Revolution. There was a huge conflict between the old aristocracy that tried to maintain a feudal system in Europe, and the emerging capitalist bourgeoisie. As a result, large chunks of people tried to emigrate out of Europe, and South Africa, unfortunately, became a haven for quite a few of these types of people. Also, one found that with the influx of a large white settler population, there was a need to control the indigenous people as well. That need translated itself not only in terms of conquering the black people who were living in and around the settler positions in South Africa, but also in regulating their movements and their whole lives. Basically, the indigenous people during this period were pastoral. They had a pastoral economy; they lived off the land, they were a free nation in the sense that they were not introduced into a money economy; they were absolutely free in that sense.

With the advance of capital and industrialism in South Africa, the settler regime had to coerce the local people into the economy. But the local people were not quite interested in the new type of economy that was set up for them. They resisted as much as they could and were annihilated. Numerous wars were waged against indigenous people stage by stage--they kept pushing the black people across the river all the time. It went on and on until eventually one found that the African people were herded into reserves. Now these reserves were not something new; they were areas where the African people actually dwelt. These were areas into which they were herded and were called native reserves. They were set up in the early nineteenth century, long before the Afrikaaner Nationalist Party began to rule in South Africa. This was the work of the British colonialist regime. One can say very safely today that the reserves set up by the 1913 land acts are almost exactly the same as the Bantustan homelands that they have today. There is probably a 2 percent shift in land area, but basically the reserves are as identical both in situation and land area as they were in 1913.

What I am trying to demonstrate is that the attitude and position of the black people in South Africa is determined or has been determined by the settler regime and by the economy. In 1913 the African people were driven into these reserves because cheap black labor was needed. If one recalls, gold and diamonds were discovered in 1896, and because these minerals were very deep in the ground, it required a tremendous amount of labor to extract them profitably. To extract them, the settler regime had to look to the indigenous black people for their labor. As

I said earlier, the black people were not prepared to work in the mines; they were not prepared to go down into the bowels of the earth to earn a living. They didn't have to. They had the land, they had the cattle, and they lived quite happily and contentedly. But to force them into the mines, the blacks had to be herded into the reserves. Not only was the settler regime happy about that, but they began imposing a tax on the black people in the country. There were taxes on the number of huts--it was called a hut tax for each person living in the hut; they had to pay a tax on each domestic animal; they had to pay taxes on the dogs. There were numerous other suchlike taxes. The whole point about these taxes was not to get revenue, but to coerce these people into a money economy. In order to pay the taxes, they had to work. And the only work that they could get was in the mines and on the farms of the white settler regime. This is how the black people became integrated and involved in the money economy of South Africa. As a result of this, one found that the laws in South Africa began to change.

I just picked up a code from a commission held in 1922, which, after having sat for many, many months on this matter, said that the natives should only be allowed to enter the white areas which are essentially the white man's creation when they are willing to enter and administer to the needs of the white man; and, they should depart therefrom when they cease to minister. Now that report is still valid. Today you have the same position where the African people have to commute both from the homelands and the Bantustans and the locations and minister to the needs of the white regime in South Africa.

Having done so, they have to go back to their ghettos. In order to do that and regulate it, you have your pass laws, your influx control, and numerous other laws. But side by side with this the black people began to realize the nature of the oppression and the nature of the oppressors. They began to realize that the source of the problem was the white man. They did not originally, perhaps, identify it in the manner we do today. But they saw the white man as the oppressor, and he symbolized oppression to them. There were a number of pitched battles, the great battles of Natal; the great battles in what is known today as Lesotho. Huge kingdoms were destroyed by the white regime and yet the battle continued as far as the black people were concerned.

The leadership was annihilated and there was a long period of consolidation amongst them. The church movement in South Africa, the missionary movement, began to fill the vacuum that was left by the traditional leaders--by the traditional kings of the black people at that time. However, the church and the missionaries filled the vacuum and began leading and enunciating the demands of the black people during this early period of the struggle. I am talking of the early twentieth century. Gradually there developed a tendency, a type of movement in South Africa that said one must petition the queen, the great white queen. The prime minister was petitioned and numerous delegations were created. Blacks began getting involved in native representation councils. Such efforts were made by them under the control and guidance of a liberal element which took control at that time.

But after World War II, the tremendous euphoria that swept Europe began to seep into South Africa as well. Black people were not directly involved; they did not experience this great fervor for freedom, this great need to fight fascism. They did not identify both of these systems as one. Slowly but surely, the people began to realize that what was going on in Germany and Europe was very much the same as what was happening in South Africa. They saw it and for the first time black liberation movements began to double up; in this way, they became independent of the liberal elements in the country. In about the forties great movements took place amongst the people, where a number of liberation movements and organizations began to band together to identify their problems in terms of a common enemy. Consequently, these groups formulated a strategy against oppression in South Africa. But once again the big and powerful business at that time, the Chamber of Mines, together with the church movements and the liberal elements, began to form an alliance to deal with this emerging independent black liberation movement.

Subsequently, in the fifties, up until the midsixties, the liberation movements were again under the control of the liberal element in South Africa. The type of struggle in which the black people began to engage was a sort of diluted, diffused struggle which misdirected, misled, and rechanneled their efforts against the enemy. Blacks began to involve themselves in a number of what they realize today as useless, futile, and sterile activities. They got involved in huge, mad, defiant campaigns and pass law burnings, which eventually led to tens of thousands of people being arrested. Leaders were banned and exiled. In 1960, the situation eventually came to a boil with what was known as the Sharpeville incident. The Sharpeville incident was a real watershed--the whole black nation almost spontaneously rose against oppression. It is true that initially the move was to make the South African system ungovernable, but once the momentum started with the people, the state also unleashed tremendous repression against them. Hundreds were killed and shot. Sharpeville 1969.

Nobody talks about all the other killings that took place in Durban, Cape Town, Johannesburg, Victoria, and the Eastern Cape. I remember 1960 very clearly because we were involved in Natal, and we tried to join the people marching down from the African locations. We were in the forefront of this march on the prisons when suddenly the tanks appeared. We were lucky to be saved, but hundreds of others were just shot down. This is the sort of activity that people were involved in--it was spontaneous, not quite organized. They did not identify goals; they did not identify methods of struggle, and once again this great urge to liberate themselves failed in 1960. I want to mention here that it was a watershed year in South African politics and liberation movements. But one of the terrible things about the 1960 events was that there was a twofold effect on both the liberation movement and South African society in general. It gave the ruling class the opportunity and rationale to introduce more and more repressive laws into the country.

I am certain Sydney Kentridge will refer to the laws between 1960 and 1970. There were so many laws, so many repressive laws, being introduced during that period that I think if one spent a lifetime trying to trace and trip over these things one wouldn't even finish. That was the reaction of the state in the decade of the sixties. The authorities came down with a very, very heavy hand and the people were virtually mowed down. The leadership, the organizations, the liberating organizations were banned and people were forced to flee the country. Regarding the leadership: You have a period of virtually no political activities in the country during that particular decade.

However, it was not enough to keep people quiet. A new generation was born. A new generation realized that they were not going to be born again and, in 1976, they participated in the Soweto uprising. Significantly this time it wasn't the old people, the mothers, fathers, workers, and brothers that were involved. This time we found very strikingly that it was the young students--an almost world phenomenon in the sense that in the late sixties the same resurgence was in the United States and especially France and Great Britain. Young people began to question, began to revolt, and began to test the systems under which they were living. South Africa, too, did not escape this, except that there it was the black students who rose, not directly against anything international, but the students who fought against Bantu education. They said that Bantu education was gutter education and they were not going to put up with it any longer. Since 1976, there has been constant turmoil and unrest in the educational system.

Now, that leads us to what is happening today in South Africa. The 1976 events did not quite boil over. The state responded in many ways, but not in the same fashion as it did in the 1960s. It was a bit more circumspect as you would see with the sort of sentences--judgments-- that the courts passed since the sixties, in the seventies, in 1976, and today. There has been a perceptible change in the responses from both the legal system and the judiciary. I want to maintain that these changes--these responses from the legal system, from the judiciary--were responses to the challenges that the liberation movement of the black people have thrown to the white ruling minority in South Africa.

Before I deal with the responses of the judiciary and the legal system, I want to state briefly the sort of responses that the white minority government is making in South Africa today. President Botha talks a lot about reforms and changes. President Reagan is happy that

Botha is talking about reforms. But we, the black people in South Africa, maintain that whatever responses the Botha government responds to--it is not to the demands of the black people. The government's responses are to the demands of big business and international capital.

You will find that before Botha's famous January 1986 declaration he was going to do away with pass laws; he was going to relax influx control; he was going to change certain laws affecting small businesses. The fact that he wants to give citizenship to the urban African-- these are not the responses or demands that the black people put forward. These were the demands almost totally and to the letter of the demands that big business, big corporations, both national and international made to Botha. It is significant that these demands were almost similar to those made in 1960 after the Sharpeville incident. Today one finds big business and international capital making certain demands on Botha and that he is responding. These responses of course do not answer the problems of the black people. Hence, you still have the unanswered questions, the unanswered demands, and the black people are, even today, risking their lives in search of their own freedom.

I promised that I was going to deal with the responses of both the judiciary and the legal system in South Africa, and I want to do this very briefly because I feel that Mr. Kentridge is going to take up the subject. I must say that there is a definite relationship between the state and level of political consciousness, the level of militancy of the black people, and the response of the judiciary in South Africa. During the early sixties, the judges virtually patted themselves on the backs when they dished out sentences of twenty years to life for simple political offenses. Nobody got less than twenty years in the early sixties. But slowly we find that with change, with the growing mobilization of the people, the judiciary also changes, keeping in step mainly with the ruling class in the country. One found that in 1976 the sort of statements and acts that the students were involved in only drew sentences of up to a maximum generally, this is not absolute, of about five to eight years. But earlier, similar acts and offenses would have drawn between twenty to twenty-five years. One would find today that people are beginning to say and do things for which in the sixties they probably would have been hanged. The judiciary is changing; they are responding. In 1974, I remember quite clearly, one comrade from Robben Island completed his sentence and returned home. But a day before he returned, he was served with a banning order. The minister believed that he was still continuing with his so-called subversive activities. Despite the fact that he was on Robben Island for ten years and, during the last three or four years the prison authorities considered his behavior so good that they graded him A, he was declared to be engaged in subversive activities.

This action was challenged in court and the court held that the minister had a right to ban this person. The matter then went to the appellate division, which upheld the earlier court's findings. But only last month, we found that because of changing circumstances again the judiciary leaned over backwards and found that the ministers had no right in similar cases of banning people. The Jack Ensuli[1] case is a classic example. Many, many people today are being unbanned on that basis. The judiciary is beginning to feel brave and hand down more liberal judgments. I maintain that the judicial system in South Africa is not doing this out of moral conviction or any sense of philanthropy or

---

[1] The spelling is phonetic.

love of justice. Most of these people on the benches were the people, who had a tradition of South African justice, that is, one kind of justice for blacks and another kind of justice for whites. These are the people today who are changing.

They are changing, I maintain, because they know that change will arrive in South Africa in their own lifetimes and they want to be on the right side of the line. They want to establish legitimacy in the legal system of South Africa, and they are beginning to lay the foundations. The state, too, has begun to encourage, turn a blind eye, or nod approval to this change in the judiciary because any evidence of liberalism, reform, or change in the judicial system also gives a lot of credibility to the white minority regime. This regime needs this credibility both for its national white minority and for international consumption. South Africa needs credibility, and the sort of judgments handed down today augurs well both for the state and the judiciary. With that I want to rest.

MR. KENTRIDGE: Mr. Chairman, ladies, and gentlemen, you will have noticed that the title given to this discussion is a very open-ended one: "The Role of Law and Lawyers in South Africa." Of course it is subject to an unexpressed qualification which I will come to, but for the most part I think this must be said at once: The role of lawyers in South Africa is very much what it is in the United States or in any advanced industrial state. Most of our cases are about contracts, reports, insurance, or banking. In good times they are about mergers and acquisitions and in bad times about bankruptcies. We are sufficiently advanced to have the same range of criminal offenses that you have in the United States, and, in the criminal courts, lawyers act as criminal lawyers do anywhere. But of course, what this title really means is the role of law and lawyers in an apartheid state. I suppose this panel is about the role of law and lawyers in protecting the individual against the apartheid state, or one might say in fighting or opposing apartheid. I certainly do not propose to give a lecture on the South African legal system or on the political system. You have heard an eloquent historical conspectus of how South Africa has become what it is. But there are certain fundamental aspects which perhaps I must mention if you, as American lawyers, are to understand both the limitations and challenges of the work of the South African lawyer.

The first thing that I am sure you all know is that South Africa is not a federal state. It is a parliamentary state in the sense that parliament has unlimited legislative power. South Africa is not controlled by any federal system; it is not controlled by any bill of rights or by an entrenched constitutional equivalent. The black majority in the population, and it is a large majority, about twenty-two to twenty-four million as against four to five million whites, has no vote. In other words, it is a parliamentary system subject to most of the people not being able to vote. The enactments of parliament, since 1948 particularly, have embodied a code of undisguised racial discrimination. This is supported by a body of security laws.

You have just heard about some of them, and you have heard about them from someone who has been at the sharp end. These laws give the executive in South Africa powers which are perhaps without parallel in any state that regards itself as part of the Western community of nations. These security laws were developed from the 1960s onwards, and I won't try to summarize them for you. As Sonny Venkatrathnam has said, it is virtually impossible to state them all, but let me give you a particular example which is perhaps the most significant: the laws relating to detention without trial.

Under this law, the police may detain and hold any person that they believe is engaging in terrorism or subversion or possessing information about terrorism or subversion. They need not charge the detainee, they need not justify the detention to any court, and they may hold the person concerned indefinitely for the purposes of interrogation. And indefinitely means indefinitely--it sometimes lasts as much as a couple of years. During this time the person detained has no right to see a lawyer, private doctor, or, indeed, anyone other than a government official. It was being held in this sort of detention that Steve Biko met his death. The statute provides, what is more, that no court has jurisdiction to pronounce upon the validity or legality of the detention. Similarly, under acts of this sort by pure executive order without judicial review, the ministers concerned may ban an organization, may ban a newspaper, may prohibit people from attending meetings, or prohibit them from living anywhere except in a designated place. The constitutionality of the act of parliament which gives these powers cannot be challenged in any court.

Again, by way of introduction, let me just say a word about the courts. Save for the fact that we have no juries, we have more or less inherited the English common law system of criminal and civil procedure. The judges in South Africa, that is, the superior court judges, are appointed by the government. They cannot be removed once they are appointed, and by convention they are appointed from the ranks of senior advocates. Nonetheless, in spite of this convention that they are appointed from the ranks of senior advocates, there has been ample scope for appointments of judges on political grounds. Now fortunately, not all the judges have been appointed on political grounds. There are many who have been appointed on merit and there still are. It is not always easy to see the distinction. I remember once hearing a former minister of justice in South Africa, a rather cynical man, saying at a gathering of lawyers that he, in his time, had made many political appointments to the bench. The trouble, he said, with the political appointment to the bench is that after he had been there for two weeks he imagined he had gotten there on merit.

Well, what can one do in the courts with such a system? What can one appeal to if there is no constitution and no bill of rights? The fundamental answer is that one tries to appeal to the Roman Dutch Common Law. The Roman Dutch Common Law System of South Africa is an extremely liberal system. It is a system which does not recognize discrimination. It has a presumption of equality before the law. The only problem in South Africa, of course, is that this is subject to parliamentary legislation. So the rule, of equality under law in South Africa, is that there is prima facie equality under law--save to the extent that parliament has done away with that equality. Certainly over the last thirty or forty years, parliament has not been backward in doing away with that equality. Well now, what are lawyers able and unable to do under the system?

First of all, let's take criminal cases. Apart from the ordinary criminal case of what anyone would regard as a crime, there is a great mass of cases from treason down to cases of prosecutions of persons who are charged because they have breached a banning order. Perhaps they attended a social gathering when they were under their banning order, which they were not entitled to do. One has this mass of criminal trials and, of course, very often part of the duty of counsel is to defend these cases. Sometime ago I heard a talk by an expert in Russian law about the Russian criminal law system. What he told us was that in the Soviet Union, in criminal trials, the conviction rate is 98 percent. He was entirely unable to account for the 2 percent acquittals. Well, in South Africa it is not like that. In many ways the system is loaded against the accused for various reasons which I won't go into now, but which we can discuss later. One does get acquittals and one even gets acquittals in treason trials. I say "even" for this reason: Lord Macauley, writing in his history of England about the reign of James II, said that an acquittal in a treason trial is always a defeat for the government of the day. I think that is still true. And it is extraordinary that in South Africa people sometimes do get acquitted in treason trials. That happened very recently in a major treason trial in which the government had set great store by reason of the advocacy of counsel in the case and the rulings of an outstanding judge who happened to be presiding. The accused, who were the leaders of a South African political organization known as the United Democratic Front, were all acquitted.

One of the functions of lawyers is to defend in these trials and, for the most part, there is counsel available to handle these defenses. What else do lawyers do? In spite of the absence of a bill of rights, one can, by making use of the common law, positively attack administrative and executive measures of the government. One starts with the presumption of equality. Now just let me give one or two examples in the 1950s. For the first time in the Cape, the government, which is still the present government, introduced apartheid on trains in the Cape peninsula where there had not previously been apartheid. Carriages were set aside for different races and that was challenged in the courts. It was challenged successfully because at that time there was no statute which permitted the government to discriminate in transportation. Well, that was soon cured. In 1953, in South Africa as in the United States, the separate but equal doctrine disappeared, but the disappearance was in a different direction. There was a very simple statute passed in South Africa called the Reservation of Separate Amenities Act, and it stated that any governmental or municipal institution could provide separate amenities in transport or in anything else. It specifically provided that the separate amenities need not be equal. A great deal of litigation was saved in the courts.

Similarly, in our common law, there is a form of common law due process which says that when an executive authority is about to take action which will prejudice an individual, they first have to give the person a hearing. And again in the 1950s when these banning orders were imposed on people, there was a challenge to them because the people who were banned had not been given a hearing. This challenge was again upheld in the courts. It was upheld because the statute which provided for banning did not expressly exclude the right to a hearing. There again it was quickly repaired by parliament. An act was passed simply saying that this could be done without any prior hearing. Although they did say that when this was done the minister had to give reasons to the person who was banned, the person concerned could then make representations as to why the ban should not continue. In my experience of these cases, I have known no instance where the representations were successful.

Of course another way in which measures can be attacked is simply by a process of statutory interpretation. One goes to court and argues that a statute which gives vast powers on the face of it to the government should be interpreted in a limited way. Again, there are many examples. I have indicated that there are the provisions for detention without trial, and there is a provision which says that no court may inquire into the validity of a detention made under this statute. What happens when someone has been banned under the statute or detained, but reasons have not been given? Such cases have been taken to court. How does one meet the provision which says that the court may not inquire into the validity of a detention under this statute? Well, one does it because the courts have held by a process of strict interpretation that the words "detained under this statute" mean detained in accordance with the provisions of the statute. So that if the provisions of the statute are not regarded, then say the courts, it is not a detention under the provision of the statute. These are all limited ways of dealing with apartheid in the courts. Certainly there is no way in South Africa in which lawyers can bring the system down, destroy it, or revolutionize society in the way in which lawyers have been able to do in the United States. This is very theoretical.

I thought perhaps that just to give you the flavor of practice in South Africa, I might mention a few cases in which I personally have been concerned. I have always found when I have read the memoirs of prominent lawyers, they only have space in their 1,800 pages or so to deal with the cases which they won. Well, the cases I am going to mention are all cases which I lost. You mentioned Mrs. Mandela. She is the wife of Nelson Mandela, who was for many years under a banning order. The order provided that she had to live in a small village in the Orange Free State--nowhere else. She had to live there for many years, and then her house was burned down by hostile elements. She believed they were not unconnected with the security police. I have no reason to think her wrong. Mrs. Mandela left that place and went back to her home which was just outside of Johannesburg. A few months ago the government then amended her banning order to say that she could live anywhere in South Africa except in the Johannesburg area where her own home was. Now, when this new order was made, no reasons were given. The minister relied on the reasons he gave for the original banning order he had made previously. In that order the reasons were simply a repetition of the statute. He said: "I banned Mrs. Mandela because in my opinion it is desirable in the interests of public order that she should be banned." We took this to court and argued that this sort of reason was not a reason. If a minister can ban a person in the interests of public order, then he is not giving a reason if he simply says I banned you because I consider it necessary in the interests of public order.

This came before a judge in Johannesburg--I don't know how to categorize him--let me say he was an amiable judge. What I thought was a fairly good argument didn't find favor with him and he dismissed this application. However, we noted an appeal and only two or three weeks ago the court in South Africa, hearing an appeal in a very similar case, said the minister's attitude was wrong; that these so-called reasons weren't reasons at all. It followed that the bans were bad in law. And this, of course, applied to everyone whose banning order was given in such terms. Here we come to something that Sonny Venkatrathnam was talking about. If this had happened in the fifties or sixties or even the early seventies, this decision of the court would have been immediately followed by a change in the law or a change in the terms of the banning order. There is reason to believe now that this will not happen. I am sure it is because we have a different political climate.

Let me give you a second case. This was one in which I could not lose. Under the recent emergency regulations, it was provided that any policeman, even the rawest recruit could, without warrant, arrest any person if he, the policeman, believed that the arrest was desirable in the interests of maintaining public order. There was another regulation which was designed to deal with the militant schoolchildren of the black townships around Johannesburg. This regulation provided that during school hours every child at a black school had to be in the classroom. They could not even be in the playground. One day the police came to a school of about 700 children and there were large numbers of children milling about the playground. The police came in force; they brought in an army detachment, and they arrested every child in the school. Not only those who were in the playground, but those who were actually in the classrooms or the library doing their work. The police went and pulled them out of the classroom and they arrested all the teachers as well.

The police took them to a station and then to prison where they were going to be kept for two weeks. Well, we were able to mount an urgent application to court. We went before a judge on a Saturday afternoon and the police were represented by counsel; they said that they had changed their minds and had decided to release all these children. It was said, however, that this decision had absolutely nothing to do with the fact we brought an application to court, and we must not think for a moment that it did. But the students and teachers were all released. The proceedings were then adjourned on the question of costs. Was the government going to be liable to pay our legal costs? And, of course, the argument on costs was going to raise the question of whether the police, even under this drastic legislation, had the right and the power to arrest a whole school. This was argued only a few weeks ago. My submission was a simple one. It was that although the police had this enormous power to arrest anyone whose arrest and detention they thought necessary to maintain public order, the regulations did not provide for collective punishment or the taking of hostages or anything of that sort. The argument was that at least the policeman concerned had to apply his mind to the case of every individual who was arrested. To arrest people who were obeying the law and who were trying to do what the regulation wanted them to do, namely, to stay in their classrooms and work, could not be possible even under this regulation. I should have thought that the contrary was virtually unarguable.

In England in the 1890s there was a famous or perhaps I should say notorious chancery judge of whom it was said that before him no case was certain and no case hopeless. I came before a judge of this type, except that in his court no case on behalf of the government is hopeless and no case against the government is certain. And on some basis which I am still at a loss to explain, the judge held against me. He said, no, the statute says it is the policeman's view that counts, and if the policeman believed that it was necessary to clear out the classrooms in the interest of public order, so be it.

I will tell you about another case. Let me start with a bit of civil law. I don't know whether those who practice in the intellectual property field have heard of the type of proceeding which in England is called an Anton Rupert. It developed in the intellectual property field. Let us say you were the owner of the copyright of music cassettes and that there was someone pirating them. You had evidence that the pirate had all these cassettes in a little shop somewhere. You knew that if you went to court for an injunction or a seizure order, all the infringing cassettes would have gone out the back door by the time notice was given. So a procedure was developed in England which also came to South Africa. If you were in this position, if you gave notice the evidence would disappear, and, if it was essential evidence, you could go to a judge *ex parte*, have a hearing in camera, and get an order from the judge. The attorney would then go with the order in his hand, enter the premises, and in terms of the order be permitted to search and take possession of the real evidence.

I then had a case instructed by a young solicitor. This was in the Eastern Cape of South Africa in a town called East London. He had a brilliant idea. In an action for damages, which was just about to start, the solicitor was representing six young black men who had been arrested by the police in East London. While they were there for interrogation, they had been subjected to electric shock torture. The basis of it was this: Here, we said, was a strong prima facie case on affidavit that these people had been tortured. It was supported by medical evidence; doctors who had seen them immediately afterwards discovered marks which looked like electrical burns. It was our position that if the police had noticed, certainly by the time the case came to trial, the electric shock apparatus would be nowhere to be found. We said this was essential evidence.

We came to court and the court heard us in camera, gave an order that until judgment the proceedings were to remain secret, and then gave a number of valuable findings. First of all, the court held that this proceeding was available against the state and against the police. There was no reason why it should be limited to cases like copyright cases. Further, they said, yes, we had made out a strong prima facie case. Further, and this was extremely interesting, they held there was good reason to fear that if the police got notice they would do away with the apparatus if it existed. But then they nonetheless rejected the application. If this were a class I would call on someone to tell me why, but let me tell you why. The court said the other element of this procedure was that the evidence you want to seize must be essential evidence. They said that meant evidence without which you could not launch your case or win it. Then said the court, our case, on the papers with the medical evidence there, was so strong that we did not need this remedy. You can judge for yourself whether this was a new refinement of legal learning or a failure of judicial nerve. I will express no opinion at all on that subject.

This is just an example of the sort of things we do or try to do. The question often arises: Is there any point in it if you cannot bring down the system--is it necessary and useful to do what one can in the courts? Of course people have different answers to this. It may be, as Sonny Venkatrathnam has suggested, that some of the victories when there are victories in the courts are issued in order to give a spurious respectability to the apartheid system. But these questions I don't think are for me to answer, certainly not at this stage. If there is an answer it is one which should perhaps be given by those who either do or do not want our services as lawyers. Thank-you.

PROFESSOR HENKIN: I suppose you, like me, wonder what I am doing here. I think the people who organized the panel thought that Columbia ought to show the flag, so Jack Greenberg and I are here to show the flag. Perhaps also the United States, although we did not invent the term, is the country of the sandwich. Therefore you have gotten the beef and Jack and I provide the bread.

I am not a South African expert. As you heard, I am an academic, a United States citizen, and I like to think of myself as concerned with human rights. I won't even comment on what the American lawyer might do about this problem. As I was sitting here, I saw the presence of a member of the panel in what is now a famous case among a very small coterie of lawyers called the *Filartega* case. And that, some of you may know, is a case where an American court gave a judgment against a foreign official for torture. I was wondering somehow if we could ever get a suit against some South African under the *Filartega* principle. I have often thought of that as a freak case, and I suspect even with judges like Will Feinberg and others we won't get very much of that here.

I was going to comment a little on what you have heard from the perspective of international human rights, and say a word on United States policy on human rights in South Africa. About South African apartheid from international perspectives, there really is not much to say. Apartheid is the most condemned violation of human rights, more so than Hitler, if you are talking about the number of condemnations and the number of condemnors. It has been condemned by everybody; in the United Nations for example, there isn't a day that goes by in which some organ does not come out with a resolution against it. The not so radical American Law Institute has tentatively approved, and I am confident it will approve, a rule in the Restatement which is that consistent patterns of racial discrimination are violations of international law--customary international law--binding on all states whether or not they are parties to any particular agreement. I don't know whether in South Africa one can try and invoke international law in the courts, but I suspect that in a country with parliamentary supremacy one would not get too far. In addition, apartheid is the subject of a special convention. It is called a Convention on the Crime of Apartheid. The only other subject, the only other human rights violation which has earned similar status, is genocide. So we have a convention on the crime of genocide and a convention on the crime of apartheid.

Apartheid has been the object of sanctions by the United Nations Security Council which no other violation of human rights has ever really had. Other sanctions against South Africa are recommended regularly by the overwhelming majorities in the United Nations General Assembly. The only reasons that they don't get enforced or implemented are of two kinds: The opposition of Western developed countries who do not want to be told not to trade with South Africa, and perhaps some subversion by developing countries who cannot afford not to trade with South Africa, or who think they cannot. Thus, you have a clear statement on apartheid by the international human rights movement.

As I thought about this, it struck me that there is one problem talking about apartheid. We tend to equate it with segregation in the South and to some extent there is good reason for that equation. But then I heard our two South African speakers. It struck me that somehow apartheid becomes not merely a violation of the principle of nonseparation or the principle of discrimination on account of race, and not merely a violation of the principle valued so much for forty or sixty years, which we called separate but equal. But somehow it drags into it a violation of every other kind of human right that the international movement has recognized. In particular, when Mr. Kentridge spoke, it seemed that the Universal Declaration of Human Rights which, by the way, speaks repeatedly about racial discrimination, is the most widely disseminated principle in the human rights lexicon. In addition, every one of those rights seemed to be something that gets violated in South Africa in relation to, or because of, the apartheid problem. I went down the list and I found torture. You have heard Mr. Kentridge talk about it; inhuman treatment and punishment, arbitrary arrest, detention, or exile. I am quoting from an international instrument; you can make the application. Arbitrary interference with privacy, family, home, correspondence, freedom of movement and residence, the right to leave and return to one's country, the right to a nationality--a subject which did not come up, but which may come later--the terrible so-called homelands program where people born and having lived in South Africa for generations are told they are not nationals of South Africa, but of some other place they have never heard of. The right not to be arbitrarily deprived of one's nationality, the right to marry someone of your own choice, to own and not to be deprived of property, and freedom of opinion and expression.

It is a long list. The right to peaceful assembly and association, the right to take part in government, and the right to equal access to public service. The statement in the international instrument said the will of the people, *the* people, not only a few people, shall be the basis of the authority of the government, equal voting for all by universal suffrage and equal suffrage, free choice of employment, equal pay for equal work, just and favorable remuneration, an adequate standard of living, and education directed "to the full development of the human personality." It ought to be clear to us that we are not merely talking about a system which separates on account of race, but which, as a result of commitment to that principle, finds itself violating virtually every other item in the international lexicon.

Now, the other thing that strikes me as I listened to the speakers is a kind of irony. In South African tradition and perhaps in relation to 15 to 20 percent of its population, there is the appearance and some reality of a Western liberal democracy. If you are white and you do not get involved with these terrible dirty problems, then you live almost as you would in a European country. I say European rather than American because the system of government is more like a parliamentary democracy on the Westminster model, not on ours. South Africa has on the whole an independent and honest judiciary; they have freedom of religion apparently. To my surprise on a long ten-day visit, I say and know from other sources, there is quite a free press-- at least the English press. The press is not in those respects an embarrassment to either its British or Netherlands antecedents, and could be a model of democracy for Africa.

Feeling good about that, I thought it means first of all you do not have to do very much. All you have to do is abolish a few small things and you have a system of government operating. Then I thought that could probably be said about the South of the United States in antebellum America. Except for the slaves, the whites lived not too differently from the way I described.

Now 100 years have elapsed and I am not saying that we had the same kind of freedoms for the whites in those days, but you essentially had a decent "white society" with a big slave population. So that is about where we stand. South Africa is certainly the most condemned nation today, and I suppose we as Americans can only add that it will continue to be condemned until there is a radical change. That radical change cannot come about unless the whole system of apartheid is dismantled. I am afraid it cannot happen unless there is universal suffrage or political participation. I speak for the rest of us here except for our two South African friends whom I assume are as equally outraged, but also equally ignorant and equally helpless as to what to do about it. Many of us have thought about the kind of universal political participation which can come to South Africa and which would be internationally acceptable. I do not have the answer to that.

I think our first speaker was right in telling us that the South African regime is responding to international pressures more or less in some measure. But they have not been responding to the internal forces and to the demands of blacks. Of course, I cannot say about that. I should say the international covenants on this subject are not very clear. They do not prescribe parliamentary democracy; there may be different models which would be equally acceptable as equal participation. Any model must respect and insure human rights in the sense that it is articulated in the universal declaration. What could the United States do? We don't know. The U.S. policy is groping. As was said, constructive engagement is a sham, and I think it is now discredited--certainly in most quarters in the United States. The U.S. policy on human rights has evolved, and it has evolved even within the years of the Reagan administration. But I think South Africa is going to be a touchstone of our human rights policy. The administration has announced its support for democracy, and the issue of apartheid is an issue of democracy. We now begin to take credit for Haiti and the Philippines, and the question is what are we prepared to do for South Africa?

At the least, it seems to me that the United States government has to press South Africa to move in a meaningful way. I suppose it is your job and mine to press our government to press the South African. If we don't, for that time in the future, we will have few friends and little influence on the African continent or on what happens in South Africa. I think as lawyers we probably have to be ready to help the process. We can be a voice and a force for human rights for all of South Africa's inhabitants. I happen to hear occasionally of Americans who wonder what will happen to the whites when the change comes in South Africa. That is a problem which, perhaps because most of us in this room are white and because we think that even whites are entitled to human rights, may be of some concern to us. This morning's *Times* had a troubling little item at the bottom of the editorial page for those of you who read it. Look at it and run across the number of casualties that might come about during a violent change in South Africa. The person to whom the reporter spoke said: "Aren't you being very sentimental?" Well, perhaps we are sentimental, and certainly most of us would hope that change would come in South Africa without bloodshed. When it comes to that, we can only say that if you want to have a South Africa which conforms to international human rights and which approximates something like the kind of rights we believe in, in the United States, we have to talk now about human rights after there has been a change in the South African regime. If in the course of x years, x being a small number, we could move the South African regime towards an authentic democratic human rights regime, we would all be in a stronger position to insist or at least ask that the same kind of thing continue whenever other kinds of change take place, whether there or somewhere else.

So as lawyers, I think all we can do is keep the issues boiling. We can educate ourselves and each other. To some extent, we have had both our South African speakers here as educators to our students; perhaps we can provide assistance for them insofar as they ask for it. Above all, we can press the United States government to help bring about peaceful changes in South Africa.

QUESTION: Do lawyers face personal risks for participating in political cases?

MR. KENTRIDGE: Well, I think for white lawyers virtually none. But black lawyers who have taken part in political cases have been at risk, for example, by being subjected to banning orders themselves. In fact, there have been a couple of cases where they have been murdered--by whom, one doesn't know. But there's a big difference between the position of white and black lawyers. Perhaps Sonny Venkatrathnam has a view on that.

MR. VENKATRATHNAM: I don't think I can add much to that except to say it depends again on the type of lawyer who is involved in defending political trials. It depends whether that lawyer is also involved in mobilizing the people in the liberation movement, and when it happens that the lawyer is both actively involved in the legal field and in the liberation movement, he exposes himself to perhaps more risks than the lawyer who gets involved only on the legal aspect. I think Mr. Kentridge alluded to people who have been killed recently by persons whom we believe are government agents. Both of the people killed were lawyers--and one had spent about ten years on Robben Island. When he came out he began defending a number of people who were charged with political offenses. Then mysteriously one day his mutilated body was found some few miles away from his home. More recently his widow was shot in front of her children in their front yard because she, too, began to be very actively involved in the struggle. She was a lawyer who represented people being tried for treason. I think there is some correlation between the sort of risks that these people face and the type of activity they are involved in--in political trials.

QUESTION: Professor Henkin commented on the inevitability of change in South Africa. If the purpose of the repressive government is to fight for its own self-preservation and these people are clearly rational, in terms of their own motivation, how can they ignore the stark inevitabilities, especially with Rhodesia as a prime example for them? How can they ignore the inevitable decay of their power with more and more repressive legislation? Why not develop a more enlightened policy to allow for a transition in which they will have even a semblance of security?

PROFESSOR HENKIN: I will ask our South African friends who are closer to the political scene to try to explain why there has not been much movement. My own impression is the question of the assumption that they are rational in the sense you use it. And the second is that they may be so determined to hold onto what they can for as long as they can that it is no longer irrational.

MR. VENKATRATHNAM: I will attempt that question, but I think that it is a problem with all human beings. You had Marcos, and Imelda wasn't satisfied with 10 pairs of shoes; she had to have 3,000 pairs. It defies all rationality you see. With the South African white regime there is the big problem that these people came from a background that was backward and conservative. They were brought up according to a Calvinist philosophy of life which they believed, and still believe, had a predestined role for black people in the country. But slowly one found that the white regime in the country has become absorbed in the economy of South Africa. Until 1960, I don't think the Afrikaaner was integrated into the South African economy. But after

Sharpeville, that big finance capital dragged these people by the scruff of the neck and got them involved in the industry in South Africa--the Anton Ruperts and others like him. Since then this Afrikaaner group has been fighting amongst itself to make reforms, but the white regime is still tied down by its own conservatism. I personally think that the Botha regime wants to change, but cannot because it is held down by its own constituency. I also think that they are being selfish; they don't want to give up what they've got. It seems to be that human weakness comes in as well. There are two forces in operation: One is the conservatism of the Afrikaaner and the white regime in the country; the other is those who are part of the modern economy. They haven't quite accommodated themselves there.

PROFESSOR GREENBERG: I just want to add that as to Imelda Marcos, I read in this morning's paper that Ferdinand Marcos said: "One must understand that those shoes were acquired over a period of twenty years and many of them were worn out."

QUESTION: Can you give us some idea of the policy of the black bar in South Africa--the size and role it is to play?

MR. KENTRIDGE: Yes, the black bar in South Africa is small, but it is growing rapidly. One of the drawbacks it has is that since the late 1950s segregated education was extended to the university level. For a long time blacks were compelled to go to inferior segregated law schools, and that made it very difficult for them to take their place in the mainstream of the bar. There are probably only about 6,000 practicing lawyers in South Africa. I would be surprised if there were more than 300 to 400 practicing black lawyers. So there is a lot of leeway to be made up, but there are a lot of people working on it.

There is now a black lawyer's association which has an educational program for practicing lawyers. That's all I can really tell you at the moment.

QUESTION: One of the obvious answers is that there is a tremendous amount of fear on the part of the white people that have a rapid change to control. I also find it a little difficult to envision exactly what the black movement would like to see happen in terms of an articulate timetable. Is anything like that constructive-- other than one man, one vote tomorrow? Has anyone proposed something that would give some clarity to change in South Africa? Is there anything systematic that would help us demand of the government the program of change that we could attempt to measure their conduct by?

MR. KENTRIDGE: Let me give a preliminary answer as a nonexpert. I am not a political expert at all. Years ago in South Africa--maybe as long as twenty years ago--there used to be a lot of constitution making. People who were in opposition, liberals and others, used to work out equitable constitutions with votes based on educational and property qualification or multiple voting. That sort of suggestion never drew the slightest response from the government. Up to this day, there is no black African person in South Africa who has a vote or who has ever had a vote in the central government of the country. Consequently, I am very diffident about purporting to speak for the black population, but my belief is that there is no serious black political leader who will be prepared to have any business at all with anything other than the democratic process as it is generally understood in the Western world. I think you are right in suggesting whites are frightened of what will happen, but the answer is that the alternatives are surely at least equally unpalatable. It is not really a question for me to answer. I think

Sonny, as I can call him a practicing politician, can answer it.

MR. VENKATRATHNAM: No, I don't think that is quite true. I don't practice politics, but it is a difficult question and I don't think anybody has a timetable. Throughout the liberation movement the black people have made tremendous sacrifices--tremendous appeals--to the ruling groups in the country. Since 1912, with the formation of the ANC, one found that the black liberation movements have been begging virtually on their knees for changes. They participated in native representative councils, Indian councils, and all these things have taught them bitter lessons--that a change by installments is no change at all--that it only prolongs the period of oppression. It makes oppression much more heavy; so much so that today the people in South Africa are beginning to learn and understand that if there has to be meaningful change, it has to come now and not later. It must not come in installments.

I will give you an example of what is currently going on. In one of the provinces of South Africa you have a man called Gatscha Buthelezi. You have probably heard of him. It is a two-faced sort of role he is playing, where he talks radical rhetoric, but functions in the same way as the other homeland leaders in the country--in the sense that he draws his pay from the government. He operates and functions like any other home Bantustan leader in South Africa. I think for some years he has been putting forward an idea of partnership--not on a national level, but on a regional provincial basis--as a test to see how a system of accommodation can operate in South Africa. He started this idea of some sort of confederalism within a regional basis, where the blacks and the whites cooperate on a provincial basis and form a government thereby. Initially, many years back, this was rejected wholeheartedly by most whites, but gradually we found that most whites in the Natal province at least supported it. They have invited all political organizations, liberation movements, the government, and white political bodies to participate, deliberate, and work out a regional solution in South Africa, and how they can accommodate one another. But the government of course has rejected this out of hand. The only two white parties I think that are participating are the progressives and the NRP. I am not certain about that, but I don't think any of the progressive black liberation movements are participating either, so that again it has shrunk to this Buthelezi group from Kwa Zulu, Inkatha, and the two white liberal parties in Natal. This sort of exercise does not appeal basically to black people in the country.

PROFESSOR GREENBERG: I want to thank our panelists. For me, it was extremely informative, terribly interesting, and useful. I think you all agree with me.

CAN TORT LAW HANDLE MODERN INDUSTRIAL ACCIDENTS?

Moderator:
ARTHUR W. MURPHY
Joseph Solomon Professor of Law in Wills,
Trusts and Estates, Columbia University

Panelists:
LUCINDA M. FINLEY
Associate Professor of Law, Yale University
STEVEN B. MIDDLEBROOK
Vice-President and General Counsel,
Aetna Life & Casualty Company
WILLIAM F. KENNEDY
Of Counsel, Hunton & Williams
GENE LOCKS
Partner, Greitzer & Locks

PROFESSOR MURPHY: Welcome to our panel entitled: "Can Tort Law Handle Modern Industrial Accidents?" It is not a very catchy title, and had Arthur Kimball not insisted on giving it a name last January, it might have matured into something like "Whither Torts" or even "Whether Torts." It may not even be a very accurate description of what will happen today. At least it would not surprise me if some of the speakers went beyond the realm of industrial accidents. We will not, however, take on the whole of tort law. The problems that are perceived in the tort law system are primarily with the system's handling of bodily injury and, to a somewhat lesser extent, physical injury to property. We will not, for example, talk about libel, slander, or invasions of privacy.

My primary role is to introduce the speakers and to act as referee; to make sure there is no hitting after the bell, no low blows, and things of that sort. As far as I can tell, this is the first program on tort law in the twenty-seven years of the Symposium. I think it is fair to say that in 1960, when the first Symposium was held, tort law was of interest largely to law professors. To be sure, we all took torts in school. Tort cases were our introduction to the legal system--our introduction to such things as case analysis. Except for automobile accident litigation, torts were probably not very important to most lawyers, and they certainly were not a major topic of conversation in the boardrooms of major industrial companies. There were exceptions. Nuclear power, for one, where the theory of unlimited liability accepted in the abstract turned out to be unacceptable, given a risk however remote it might be, of liability large enough to wipe out a major corporation. But by and large, people tended to assume that insurance would take care of them and ignored tort law.

Even the change in the early 1960s from a faultbased theory of product liability to strict liability caused barely a ripple. Contrast that bucolic scene with today: Two major corporations have sought the protection of bankruptcy courts against the impact of tort liability. A third, Union Carbide, has agreed to pay half a billion dollars to settle the claims in Bhopal, and probably can't settle that cheaply.

In recent months tort liability has been a close second to municipal corruption in the pages of *The New York Times.* There are reports galore by the American Bar Association, Congress, the Rand Corporation, and now the Reagan administration. Perhaps the best barometer of how desperate the problem is is that this administration, which is almost fetishistic about states' rights in some areas, is said to be seriously considering a federal law which would displace state tort law in many areas.

A list of the recommendations in the recent report of the administration committee is the *Report of the Tort Policy Working Group on the Causes Extent and Policy Implications of the Current Crisis in Insurance Availability and Affordability.* It gives you some idea of the major problem areas that are perceived. The recommendations are eight:

1. to retain fault as the basis for liability

2. to base causation findings on credible scientific and medical evidence and opinion (All of these are euphemisms, you understand.)

3. to eliminate joint and several liability

4. to limit noneconomic damages to a fair and reasonable amount

5. to provide for periodic payments for future economic damages

6. to reduce awards by collateral sources of compensation for the same injury

7. to schedule or reduce contingency fees

8. to develop alternative dispute resolution mechanisms

This is not, of course, a unanimous point of view. It is in marked contrast with the much longer report of the Griffin Bell Committee, as it was called--the Committee on Tort Law Reform of the American Bar Association which was issued about a year ago. The conclusion, I think it's fair to say, is that all is for the best in the best of all possible worlds. Where the truth lies is something we hope to get at this morning.

Let me now introduce our panelists in order of appearance. The first is William F. Kennedy. Bill is a graduate of Fordham College and the Law School, but although not a Columbia alumnus, he did study at the feet of Harold Leventhal when Harold was the head of OPS; therefore, we can regard him as properly trained. Bill has spent most of his professional life with the General Electric Company in a variety of legal jobs. Since his retirement he has been of counsel to Hunton & Williams. He has wide experience in the area of our discussion today--in aircraft liability and nuclear liability, which is where we met some thirty years ago. He is currently the chairman of the special subcommittee on tort law reform of the Section on Corporation, Banking, and Business Law of the American Bar Association.

Our second panelist is Stephen B. Middlebrook, vice-president and general counsel of Aetna Life and Casualty Company, a position which automatically establishes his credentials to speak on this subject. Steve is also not an alumnus of ours, but was graduated from Yale and Yale Law School. That's not so much of a defect as it would appear, since in recent years the relationship between Yale and Columbia has become nearly incestuous. For example, Barbara Aronstein Black, our new dean, tells me that we recently received a letter here addressed to A. Bartlett Giamatti, Dean of the Columbia University School of Law. We didn't know where to forward it. At least Barbara says that happened, and she is a woman of great probity--although not above gilding the lily if there is a story in it. You can ask her.

Our third panelist is an alumnus of ours, Gene Locks, a graduate of Princeton and Columbia Law School in 1962. He has been for some twenty years a member of the firm of Greitzer and Locks in Philadelphia. Gene is a trial lawyer and has represented plaintiffs in the *Agent Orange* case and in various asbestos cases. One of his fields of professional interest is product liability litigation, and he is particularly qualified to talk on our subject.

Our last panelist is Lucinda Finley, also one of ours, having been graduated from Barnard College and Columbia Law School in 1980. After a year of clerking in Philadelphia and a couple of years of practice in Washington, she joined the faculty of the Yale Law School in 1983. She is now an associate professor. Her fields of major interest include the toxic torts. All in all, I think it is a very well-qualified group.

MR. KENNEDY: Thank-you, Arthur. I should have negotiated for a later position on the panel. Like the other members here, I have spent some time on the problems--in my case going back to the development of the Price-Anderson legislation thirty years ago. Still, I didn't come here with well-formed ideas or with ready-made solutions to what are obviously a very complex set of problems. I was hoping to be able to respond to mistaken observations that some of my fellow panelists might make, but instead they are going to have the privilege of responding to my misstatements.

There is no question now that the issue is on the national agenda. There are a number of signs of that; it makes the front page of *The New York Times,* it makes the national newsweeklies, it makes the nightly TV news reports, and, not least, it is the subject of a seminar by Arthur Murphy here at the Law School. What is driving it? I think it is the failure of an assumption which motivated the movement toward strict liability, a movement which began in the 1940s and which reached a critical juncture in the early 1960s. The premise is that one could continue expanding almost indefinitely the scope of tort liability for physical injury because the liability was insurable.

Well, it turns out that the assumption "ain't necessarily so." We have seen that a system which relaxes standards of liability without controls on the amount of recoveries is putting extreme pressure on the insurance market --pressure which is forcing us to reexamine the system, and possibly go along a different route or perhaps several different routes. One can believe that the queen of England is responsible for the international narcotics trade and also believe, with some of the people quoted in the public prints, that the problems in the insurance market are the product of a conspiracy by the elders of the insurance industry. But if you look at that industry--and this is developed to some extent in the Justice Department report referred to by Arthur Murphy--you find that it is atomized and intensely competitive.

Steve Middlebrook can speak on these points much more knowledgeably than I, but it seems clear that you cannot expect that insurers will continue with practices under which a policy issued in year one will cover a claim asserted in year thirty-one, or under which a policy issued to cover acts or omissions of A will cover on a joint and several basis claims attributable to the fault of B, C, or D, even though arguably A is only five percent at fault. None of this is to suggest that we can go back to *MacPherson v. Buick* or repeal the history of the last twenty to thirty years. I do think we need to look at two strategies.

Strategy one is to try to develop on a selective basis statutory compensation systems. Such systems would provide assured expedited recovery of net economic loss, including a separate award of attorney's fees. The premise is that if there is a social judgment that certain types of physical injury ought to be compensated regardless of fault, then it will be less expensive and more efficient and fair to do it outside the tort system.

Strategy two is to tighten standards in the residual tort system, both standards of liability and measures of compensation. It is easy to toss off generalizations like this, but much harder to define the cases where a statutory compensation system would be appropriate. One of the early proposals prepared by Senator Danforth's staff would have applied it to all products, and the reaction from industry quickly made clear that that would not be workable.

I think there are cases where the concept would work. Something like it is part of the

Price-Anderson structure for nuclear accidents. The commercial aviation industry--both airlines and manufacturers--has proposed such a system. It is my understanding that the pharmaceutical industry has explored the idea at least for vaccines. It may be that the concept would work in a narrowly defined class of toxic cases, although the clutch questions there are issues of causation and the process for resolving those issues. Finally, there has been interest in the idea of Jeff O'Connell under which either party, plaintiff or defendant, could make an offer of judgment for net economic loss; if the offeree declines the offer and if, in the lawsuit, the outcome for the offeree is less favorable than the offer, then the offeree would suffer an economic penalty.

Defining the cases where a statutory compensation system might be feasible is, as I have said, difficult. But the concept should have attractions both for injured persons and for the business community. From the point of view of the injured person, the assurance of recovery, the expedition of recovery, and the separate award of attorney's fees have clear attractions. From the point of view of the business community, the possible increase in the number of claims and recoveries might be offset by savings in transaction costs, controls on the amount of recoveries, and greater predictability, and, therefore, greater insurability of aggregate costs. Let me at this point elaborate on the notion of net economic loss.

First, it does not include punitive or exemplary damages. I have long believed that the proper resolution in this area is to provide a separate regime of statutory civil penalties. Second, it implies either exclusion of claims for pain and suffering and other harms not susceptible of predictable monetary measurement or, at least, a cap on such claims. We have seen a number of states consider and in some cases enact such caps. Third, it implies a reversal of the traditional collateral source rule at least for publicly provided or employer-provided collateral sources. Fourth, it contemplates periodic or structured payments, principally on account of lost wages and medical expenses, rather than lump sum awards. Fifth, it contemplates a separate award of attorney's fees as distinct from a schedule or cap or other constraint on contingent fees.

Next, let me note that any serious proposal for a statutory compensation system would contemplate that it would supplant the tort system for claims within its scope or that, at minimum, there would have to be a binding election between the statutory claim and the tort claim.

Finally, let me say a word on the federalism issue. I think it is clear that in our national and increasingly international economy any statutory system would have to be enacted at the federal level. Apart from the imperative of uniformity, there is another compelling reason and that is the difference in the response to constitutional challenges to tort reform legislation in the federal and state courts. I think it is significant that two appeals from decisions upholding the California medical malpractice legislation--legislation challenged under the due process and equal protection clauses--were each dismissed by the Supreme Court for want of a substantial federal question. There is some basis for concern that some state courts may be more receptive to such challenges. Thank-you.

MR. MIDDLEBROOK: Arthur, my simple answer to your question: "Can Tort Law Handle Modern Industrial Accidents?" is no. Indeed, the question itself illustrates just how difficult that job has become. If we take, for example, the word "accident" in your question, I think we can illustrate this complexity. Not so long ago, in any discussion of tort law, the word "accident" would suggest a traumatic event with clear causation, involving one individual or a small group of individuals. The tort system was reasonably well equipped to assess liability under those particular circumstances; to determine causation where it had to be determined, to decide issues of negligence, to set the standards from which to assess departure from normal conduct, and to affix reasonable damages. But today, the term accident can embrace all manner of harm, and it is this expansion of the definition of accidents in our modern industrial society that I believe contributes quite substantially to the complexity and inadequacies of our civil liability system.

For purposes of discussion, we can identify perhaps four quite different categories of accident that now confront the tort system: Category one would be the "common accident," referring to traumatic events that occur regularly and pervasively throughout society. Causation is usually clear. That is to say, the question of who did what to whom can usually be determined. The standard for liability is simple negligence and is usually fairly easy to assess. Automobile accidents are a good example of what I mean by the "common accident," and so are most workplace accidents. Many of these accidents are also characterized by a community of interest that exists between the person injuring and the person injured--a factor that may have some importance in determining how these types of accidents might be handled. I will develop that thought later.

The second category is the "classic accident" with any particular type occurring relatively infrequently. Again, causation is reasonably clear or reasonably determinable, but the standards of liability in many states have evolved from simple negligence to strict liability. An example might be an individual injured by an explosion of a defective aerosol can. Here there is usually no particular community of interest between tort teaser and victim.

The third kind of accident is the "dangerous product accident"--that is, traumatic events that are caused by unavoidably unsafe products or situations where both causation and responsibility are clear, at least, in a strict liability or *res ipsa loquitur* sense. Examples would include the airplane crash and severe adverse reactions to vaccines.

Number four category is the "latent health injury." This is usually a health problem where injury is attributable to exposure to harmful substances and symptoms become manifest only over a period of time. Causation in these cases is confounded by the presence of other factors of heredity and environment, and issues of liability are also confounded by the manufacturer's uncertain state of knowledge at the time of initial exposure. Examples include asbestos, DES, birth control devices, and toxic substances found in waste disposal facilities.

There is some obvious overlap in those categories and the four of them are not intended to be all-inclusive, but they do illustrate the complexity and variety of injury and harm in today's industrial society. Perhaps it gives us some hints as to which types of accidents can best be handled by our court system and which may not be. To illustrate further the complexity of the issue, let me return to our central question: "Can Tort Law Handle Modern Industrial Accidents?" What do we mean by the tort system's ability to handle accidents? Well, the two traditional goals of the system--compensation and deterrence--immediately come to mind. (I recognize there are others.) Those goals just as quickly provoke some new tough questions. Let me talk about deterrence first. The question is deterrence of what? Traditionally, it meant deterrence of conduct harmful to others. Today it still means that, but there is now yet another very different type of deterrence, a sort of "reverse deterrence" that is playing out in our tort law. That is deterrence from the manufacture of useful products or the rendering of useful services for fear of their unavoidable consequences to a small minority of users. Examples include vaccines, recreational parks, and the practice of obstetric medicine to name just a few. What deterrence do we achieve using litigation and unlimited liability against drug companies whose products are unavoidably unsafe to a few, but absolutely essential for hundreds of thousands or perhaps millions of people? Is tort litigation an optimal deterrent for latent health problems which, as Bill Kennedy suggests, a finding as to wrongdoing may only come to light very, very long after the harm has occurred?

Compensation, another well-recognized goal of the system, raises some separate questions. Can the system really do an adequate job of compensating persons affected by latent health injuries? And is it really the best way to compensate people for repetitious, mostly minor accidental events? Is it really necessary to use the tort system at all in cases where causation and liability are reasonably clear and only the amount of damages is at issue? If we start considering other possible goals for our tort system, new issues arise. Is promptness of compensation a reasonable objective? Does that have anything to do with it? And if so, is there any evidence that the current system can deliver from that result? Is the system handling its mission adequately when fewer than half of the dollars consumed by the system make their way into the injured person's pocketbook? Is stability and slow evolution a worthwhile goal in this field? And if so, has the tort system served us well in that regard?

Those are a bunch of questions. Let me try to suggest some answers. I would contend that we may have demanded at the same time both too much and too little of our civil liability system. Too much because we have overloaded it with new tasks for which it is very poorly suited. There are clearly some classes of injury now within the system that should come out of the system. We will talk about those in a minute. We have demanded too little of the system because we have held it to too low a performance standard for handling more traditional injuries and events. Today there is an urgent need to rethink both the capacity of the system and the performance of the system.

Now, what candidates can we usefully remove from the system? One appealing group of accidents would be the common accident where causation is relatively easy to determine. Every one of us at some time will either cause an automobile accident, be injured by one, or at least be a passenger in a car involved in an accident. We might therefore come to an informed national consensus that the elaborate mechanisms of tort law simply are not needed here. Faultfinding mechanisms are neither necessary nor particularly appealing when the following conditions are met: First, when there is a community of interest between the injured and the injuring parties; that would be true, for example, when most individuals might imagine themselves as causing as well as being injured by the type of accident in question. Second, when the deterrence value of the liability system is quite low or could easily be replaced by other mechanisms.

Those conditions, I think, are each present in the auto accident area. In addition, the relatively small amounts at issue--in most cases--the desire for a speedy result and the need for a better trade-off between transaction cost and compensation--all of those things make this category of accident an ideal candidate for an alternative approach. As we all know, such an approach has been tried in many states on a limited scale. It is called no-fault automobile insurance. Recent studies by the Department of Transportation and the Institute for Civil Justice show that the objectives I have just outlined are in fact achievable. They might even be more achievable if the thresholds barring tort action, very low right now in most states, could be significantly expanded.

There is another category of accident, though stemming from the dangerous product accident, that strikes me also as a good candidate for a no-fault approach, but for different reasons. Here frequency of occurrence is low, but the total loss can be quite high. Now, why a no-fault approach? Because in those instances it will be inevitable that some people will be hurt regardless of fault, so there is really no particular deterrence effect and, except in egregious situations, there is no need to examine the standard of care with great precision. Further, in those situations, the plaintiffs rarely will have or could have contributed to their own injuries. Their comparative negligence, therefore, is not an issue. Debating fine points of responsibility in a court of law, with regard to these types of accidents, only diverts needed dollars from compensation to something called administration. Here, too, the deterrent value of the tort system in most cases strikes me as relatively low.

There have been some imaginative proposals in this regard framed for aviation accidents by Bill Kennedy and some of his colleagues. They envision essentially a two-round system of compensation recovery. The first round is designed to reimburse injured persons, antecedents' estates, and their attorneys quickly and expeditiously. It is administered before the court, solely by the airline and the airline manufacturer, splitting costs fifty-fifty. The second round is reserved for and designed to allocate liability among all other liable parties; for example, the airport, the FAA, and the suppliers to the manufacturer. Service of process is streamlined in these situations. There are economic incentives to settle rather than litigate. All of this is done in a very thoughtful way to get to the gut issues in that kind of accident without being distracted by procedural niceties--issues of joint versus several liability and the unneeded incentives of contingency fees.

What about latent health problems? Popular thinking suggests that these, too, are candidates for a new approach, such as an administrative compensation system that could operate in parallel with the tort system. Some of the problems are currently being dealt with outside the realm of the traditional system, or at least parallel to it. The Wellington facility for asbestos is one example. The *Agent Orange* settlement is another. The bankruptcy option, which you are all aware of, is still another. Alternate systems for latent health claims may hold the promise of more efficient compensation, but we should not be too ready to put a mandate on them in place of existing tort principles. At least when these complex issues first emerge, we need a careful and deliberative approach for determining causation and liability. Certainly, there is ample room for improvement in the handling of scientific evidence by the legal system as a recent Georgetown study pointed out. But the deliberative workings of our civil liability system may be as well suited to the task of considering responsibility for the new and complex types of diseases as any other system that modern man has yet invented, although I would not from this podium readily concede that there isn't a better system waiting to be invented.

Once the parameters of causation and liability become established in the latent health area of given toxic substances, I wonder if we should consider whether alternative systems can then deliver compensation more efficiently to the very large numbers of people that are usually affected by these kinds of products. There comes a point where we really don't need to relitigate every toxic tort or roll the jury dice on each determination of damages. At some point the occasionally useful incentives of exemplary damages and contingency fees not only become unnecessary in these kinds of areas, they become inappropriate and, I would argue, counterproductive.

Suppose we did have alternate mechanisms in place to address several of the types of accidents I have just described? The tort system is still there. It would still have a heavy burden to carry, and it would still need some fairly dramatic reform from within. The current crisis atmosphere that pervades public thinking can stimulate some useful prospect for reform. I could see three overarching themes that might guide us. It can be made more fair. It can be made more efficient. And it can certainly be made more predictable. I will close with some examples of how these objectives might be better accomplished.

First, as to fairness, we certainly need to reexamine the doctrine of joint and several liability. It grew up in an era where concerted action causing harm was its most frequent justification. It developed when the doctrines of contributory negligence, last clear chance, and assumption of the risk offered a quid pro quo for the crap shoot effect of joint exposure. But today those doctrines are gone. Plaintiffs now are much more fully protected through comparative negligence theories of recovery. I believe they are now in effect in every state in the union. Crap shoot justice to me makes no sense for just one side of the table. Joint and several liability is invoked in many, many more areas than traditional concerted action cases. It has become a deep pocket social policy, allowing plaintiffs to reach any well-off defendant with marginal connection to an injuring event. It plays out every day in the process of handling and settling insurance claims. The trick is to find a rich, wealthy, well-insured defendant who has some marginal connection with the loss. A municipality is a very good example of this. The whole field of finding the deep pocket defendant has become an art unto itself.

What about efficiency? Well, we need to do at least two things efficiently. One, I think we need to achieve a better balance between sums paid to injured people and amount expended on the legal fees and other administrative costs incurred, including the cost incurred by companies such as my own. We need to achieve greater equity in payment of the award itself. As to the first, it is a national scandal that less than half of the dollars the system consumes goes to compensate sick or injured people. Numerous reforms could improve this ratio and now--through studies done by groups like the Institute for Civil Justice--we are gaining a better sense of what reforms actually work and which don't. This is an area where the organized bar has a special responsibility to provide leadership.

The second component of efficiency--equity in damage awards--also deserves attention. Here we need to amend the collateral sources rule--to focus on minimizing redundant payments to injured people. In a world where first-party insurance payments have become pervasive, does duplicate payment through the tort system really make sense?

Finally, as to "predictability": Given my background, I don't need to describe for you what prompts my concern about that objective. One area of uncertainty that deserves serious attention is the handling of noneconomic loss. Compensation for intangible loss is a major component of awards and settlements, and there is little thoughtful analysis to guide those who determine the amounts to be paid. This is a fertile area for research and debate, and someone could make a real contribution to public policy by tackling this issue in a careful way.

I have in mind more than just caps on awards. That's a bit simplistic and apparently raises serious constitutional issues in at least some of our states. What may make more sense is to start by scrapping the existing common law in this area and replacing it with a more predictable but still reasonable alternative. A statute, for example, that tries to set some uniform standards for determining what type of injuries merit noneconomic recoveries and then schedules those recoveries in accordance with the severity of those injuries.

Most of these reforms are not, incidentally, just the musings of a beleaguered insurance industry. They have all been addressed in a recent federal report on insurance availability-- as authored by an interagency working group composed of ten federal agencies and the White House. With 700,000 lawyers, 7,500 legislators, and 18,000 judges in this country, we should be able to find the requisite talent to spell out these reforms in competent, effective ways. Thank-you.

MR. LOCKS: Of course, one of the benefits of being next to last, at least from one aspect of this subject, is that I can respond to some things, but before I do I think you deserve to have a little more perspective of where I come from. I was the first plaintiff lawyer in the country that obtained a punitive damages verdict against *Johns Manville* and another asbestos company. I was the plaintiff lawyer who initiated discussions with the Wellington asbestos claims facility defendants when they decided it was time to talk. I am a member of the Manville bankruptcy committee and have been one of the leading negotiators concerning the bankruptcy reorganization. Somewhere along the line about five months before *Agent Orange* was set for trial by my former evidence and civil procedure professor, Jack Weinstein, I was asked to help try the case. I was on the plaintiff's management committee and also was one of the conegotiators of that settlement.

In my other spare time, I was asked to get involved with Bhopal and Union Carbide. I won't say too much more about that at the moment, but I am sure you can appreciate some of the dynamics there. The problem I have is in deciding what to say. I have no preplanned script or statement on the issues. I can respond to the issues and I can certainly say a few things about acting on the issues. I am an actor as a lawyer. I basically represent plaintiffs who have been injured as a result of accidents or incidents, usually environmentally or occupationally located. We are talking about incidents and mass torts and the focus of where the problem seems to be today--not the traditional accidents that have existed. There is no numerocity problem.

The problem that has been created is the result of the latent disease torts like asbestos that have created a tremendous drain on the time and money of the system and the parties. Obviously, the reaction of many people to a solution is only focused on time and money. Had they done this before, there could have been many, many preventions and, in fact, with innovative and creative modifications within the system, solutions can be found. We do not need legislative mass surgery, nor do we need an abolition of the system nor elimination of the common law. That hurt me a little. There is something about the common laws that I still think we, as lawyers and citizens, have an obligation and responsibility to maintain.

Now, I guess it is probably best to indicate that when I was at Columbia I was extremely well trained for the project that I have now, since I spent almost all of my courses in taxation, corporation, international law, comparative law, and Soviet law, and I had for a well-balanced education to take a course in evidence. I had the pleasure of having a tort course with Professor Reese. I have to admit that both Jack Weinstein in evidence and Professor Reese did make the courses sufficiently enjoyable that I knew that tort law existed, but it wasn't where I started out. I have come around full circle since that time and have basically represented victims in the system. I really think that the answer of whether or not the system can handle massive incidents, not accidents, is best answered by simply saying yes, and now addressing the manner in which that could and should be done. I don't have all the answers. I can certainly debate every single issue that has been raised by both Mr. Kennedy and Mr. Middlebrook. On some I am a little more persuasive than others. We can discuss all of the aspects and I can mention a couple of them. To go back to the system itself: really, what happens if you first talk about the tort system is that you are also talking about the litigation system and the court system and the cases that are filed in court.

If you resolve those prior to coming to court, we probably wouldn't be here today, and we wouldn't be in the present posture of responding to some of the latent disease problems, such as asbestos, that have cost so much money to so many people. If you assume that, and I am not saying I don't agree because I haven't thought about it much, the four classifications of types of claims that Mr. Middlebrook suggested are what the tort system is about. I think of the first three the traumatic classic and dangerous product claim didn't seem to be a problem. Admittedly, it cost some money; admittedly, there were cases filed; admittedly, there was certain litigation; admittedly, in some aspects the litigation may or may not have been fair or it may not have been equitable or balanced, but that is not a reason to change the system. The total time and money spent on those types of claims is so different from the increase in the total amount of time and money spent generally on all types of matters in the court system. Maybe it is, but I don't think the number is justified.

I think the focus was the latent disease/latent health problem claims. Let me say to a certain extent that I have contributed substantially to creating the problem. I did it because I represented people who were injured by somebody's fault or otherwise. A person comes in and purportedly has an injury from a working or environmental situation; exposed to a product, the result is that twenty or thirty years later someone gets sick. The person is told by a doctor that in five days the statute of limitations will run out. I must help that person sue somebody. Typically, the lawyer, myself first, says we better sue everyone who made the product over a thirty or forty-year period. Asbestos, the massive problem, has occurred. I submit that the problem was initially created by the quantum of defendants and the length of the time period in which the potential liability would exist--substantially compounded by the insurance coverage problems that are created because of that time period. That was a new and difficult problem. Had that very same victim been exposed to one product, so that we don't have joint and several and/or comparative negligence and liability--whether it is over that extended period of time or not (but perhaps the extended period of time compounds it), we would not have the disaster that has been purportedly suggested to exist as a result of the number of claims. I think you have to recognize that even in a latent disease situation it is not necessarily the multiplicity of plaintiffs that causes the problem in the tort system. It is the multiplicity of defendants and their comparative roles amongst each other as well as their respective liability to the plaintiff.

From the number of multiple plaintiff lawsuits that I have been in, leaving asbestos aside at the moment--when there has been one defendant, using Bhopal or Union Carbide as an example, I don't think you are going to see a rerun of the asbestos problem. Take another incident of that nature and you won't see another rerun of the asbestos problem, but if that same incident occurred and there were fifteen potential defendants or actual defendants--that is where problems occur. If you think of that and accept it and the fact that the attorney representing the victim had to take an initial best shot at all of the possible responsible parties for the victim, you then see how there are mechanisms within the present system, precomplaint and postcomplaint that can deal with the problem. First of all, initially, in asbestos there never was an alternative to litigation. You never had a chance to call a potential or actual liable defendant and say, "I have someone who is hurt and deserving of some money. What do you think?" There was no one to talk to. There was no one to communicate with. There was no one to make any effort to avoid litigation by a fair, prompt, and reasonable settlement posture. Therefore, put it in suit and we will worry about it later. That, unfortunately, is what happened. I hope the Wellington process may develop some procedure to allow a reasonable effort in advance to resolve a case before it goes in the system. Forget asbestos for the moment. Put it to any other toxic tort--latent, massive, or single accident injury to multiple plaintiffs--single product exposure in multiple jurisdictions. If you allow that type of mechanism, you will find a substantial amount of the litigation will disappear.

You will also find if you have some device, and we don't have to debate this, not all the cases ever go to trial. The specter of erratic and inconsistent jury awards, the specter of punitive damages on a large basis, is not a problem. A single case, a single occasion, a single accident--yes. In a massive, monstrous tort situation--no. I have yet to get a single penny of punitive damages verdict from *Johns Manville* and I don't ever expect to. I have yet to believe that many of the other companies who are liable for punitive damages will ever have to pay them. I represent over 2,500 plaintiffs, and my firm has won a verdict over 100 times against many of the asbestos defendants. The consideration in settling and resolving the cases is not geared around punitive damages. I think that a precomplaint procedure, perhaps Wellington, perhaps something else, perhaps some legitimate firsthand controlled, understanding discussion with your adversaries, who are the defendants, whether they are insured, uninsured, or have an insurance coverage problem, can be meaningful and helpful. This can and will resolve many things which cost time and money.

Once you get into the litigation the system can work. Unfortunately, the lawyers and the judges don't necessarily address the problems early enough. The lawyers bring the lawsuit; the plaintiffs are not indiscriminate as has been suggested. The defense lawyers defend much more indiscriminately than the plaintiff lawyers in their choice of defendants, and no one addresses the problem because the system doesn't always provide a way to address it. For example, in any complex, massive case, an immediate judicial assignment is necessary. That judge cannot just say, "Hey, I've got a docket of 100 or 200 cases and this is just another case." The lawyers better get to that judge before responsive pleadings are even necessary to say we have a different case with a different problem, and these are the dynamics and the dimensions of it. Judges should immediately respond to that by saying let me hear about it. *Ex parte, non ex parte,* but they ought to educate themselves about the dimensions of that particular case. The minute a judge learns the dynamics and dimensions the immediate problem of voluntarily or involuntarily streamlined procedures can be done. Experienced lawyers on both sides don't necessarily like to waste time and money. We really don't like to push paper, do lots of dilatory work, or get into lots of issues where we have to make motions and arguments. Responsible lawyers on both sides can and do work out special mechanisms to avoid that. They need judicial help, a judge who makes a special rule for the case, a special order for the case, and modifies the procedures in the jurisdiction to suit the needs of that particular case. Judges also have to make themselves available at almost all times to deal with problems in the process as the discovery begins. I cannot tell you how many times in the middle of a deposition with thirty lawyers that when a witness is asked a particular question and is given some instruction, perhaps by the counsel or perhaps by one of the other twenty-nine counsel, about whether or not to do something, a quick phone call to the judge resolves the problem and the deposition goes on. If you allow each party to put the position on the records, about three hours later you may get an answer to that question or not, and you will have another hundred pages in the record. You can imagine how the costs mount and mount and mount. This is unfortunately what happened in asbestos.

What you also have to do though is to make sure, besides being available, that the judge rules on issues as they come up. You have to let the parties know the rules. The massive problem in asbestos was the fact that there were different rules in different places and no one quite knew where they were coming from until about four years later there was a verdict. They then waited three years for an appellate decision to clarify what the rules were or were not. That is wonderful but it is unfortunately a mistake of the system. A trial judge should rule if it's a matter that ought to be appealed, and the appellate court should get some expedited response so that the system can move along rather than have hundreds and hundred of cases where there is an uncertainty. The judge has to meet with and monitor the lawyers and watch what the lawyers are doing--not just know when to rule on something. The judge has to check on them regularly.

There are lots of ways to streamline motion practice. It depends on the judge. You can just call up and say, "We have a motion. Let's talk about it," or you can go through and write numerous briefs. You have the same problems where you are talking about document production. All of this goes into the pragmatic handling of the actual litigation in a way that we can get to the issue sooner. I say the system has the devices; I say the system can deal with them on a particular case. I think that the problems of the massive torts and the multiple defendants are the long periods of time. They are difficult, but workable. I would much, much rather respond to very pointed questions about some of the points raised than to try to respond to them and debate them all right now. I want to close by saying I am absolutely convinced that the system works, not as well as it could, but it does work. I absolutely think we don't trash the system because I don't see any viable alternative that is better. I absolutely don't believe that we need major surgery in this system to put it into the legislative arena, because I haven't seen too many legislative solutions of any type of tort law that have ever been effective and not administratively overwhelming to the people who are injured occupationally or environmentally by the system. I would like to debate and talk about this for hours and hours. Thank-you.

PROFESSOR FINLEY: Arthur just told me that he put me last because he thought that as an academician I would provide the voice of sweet reason on this controversial panel, but I think in tribute to my fellow panelists, they have all been reasonable. One of the possible detriments of going last was that all the brilliant things you thought you were going to say, you hear other people saying, so what can I say that will be different? I will start with what has created this perception of such a crisis right now. It is necessary to think about why all of a sudden there is such a perceived problem with the tort system before we can decide whether to get rid of it or whether to change it and, if so, how? I agree with those who say there is a crisis. Anything that is costing this much, going this slowly, and creating such a sense of frustration and arbitrariness, despite the American Bar

Association's "best of all possible worlds" report, probably isn't working very well. But the reasons it is not working very well are a lot more complex than just the tort system itself, tort law, overly litigious lawyers, arbitrary jurors, or the lack of insurance. It is a much deeper societal problem which leads me to conclude that if we were to go to a statutory compensation system, we would have an increasingly complex society with a multitude of industrial, technological, and chemical processes and, at the same time we have an increasingly sophisticated science, helping us all better appreciate some of the causes and effects of certain substances. There is both a sense that we are losing control over our environment and that maybe science can help us get it back again.

As understanding about risk increases, people are more likely to think of suing or seeking compensation rather than just saying, "Oh, well, that is fate, those are the hazards of modern life." This may underlie some of the increasing resort to the tort system be it in a toxic exposure case or a medical malpractice case--just the sense that if something goes wrong there is probably a reason--and we can figure out the reason. If so, it's not just my fate or my problem to bear, and maybe by suing and undergoing discovery we can start to unearth the cause. I, the injured victim, can deal with my fears of pain and frustration and loss of control over my life by finding an explanation. I think that is an important function of the tort system. Although the tort system is not the only system that can fulfill that function, it is a function we have to keep in mind in addition to compensation and deterrence in talking about alternatives.

My observation about the increasing complexity of society leads to some thoughts on what it is now, with the kinds of cases that are coming to the tort system, that has created such a problem. My view is essentially that the principles of the tort system are nineteenth-century principles, and they are now being applied to a twentieth-century world. The tort system rests on premises and doctrinal rules that come from premises that really were not designed for the kind of society and situations we currently have. That is not necessarily a criticism of the tort system, but it has to be a starting assumption in thinking about it and how to change it. The aspect of this twentieth-century world that doesn't really fit with the premises of the tort system is its scientific and technological complexity with extensive interactions.

The whole notion of individualized accidents between single individuals, who come together for a cataclysmic moment, and then go off on their merry ways isn't necessarily true anymore. Today we are faced with multinational and multistate activity, vast numbers of people that potentially can be exposed to and injured by products or substances or vaccines or other drugs, possible multiple numbers of defendants, regulations that affect the environment and may indeed have a lot to say on the supposed deterrent school of the tort system, as well as a lot of substances that have latent health effects. The risks, if any, don't show up until a long time after either the exposure or the marketing decision or whatever. This latter problem also raises the possibility of multiple causes, synergistic effects, genetic predisposition, and lifestyle. It all leads back again to multiple and possibly indeterminate defendants and multiple and possibly indeterminate plaintiffs. Most of the rules of tort law, be it causation, fault, standard of care, or statute of limitations were not created with any of this complex environment in mind.

That leads me to want to focus on one particular aspect of the problem that hasn't already been covered; in particular, the so-called causation controversy. I am going to talk about it in the context of latent toxic torts. My answer to the panel question: "Can Tort Law Handle Modern Industrial Accidents?" would be that it depends, as Steve Middlebrook said, on what you mean by an industrial accident. In an accident like Bhopal you don't really have the causation problems that stem from the lag time of latent effects. Although we don't know yet what is going to happen, what health effects those people are going to show in twenty years, at least with the case as it has currently been brought, we really don't have an *Agent Orange* or an asbestos situation. A case like Bhopal, which is a traumatic sudden accident, although it certainly presents size and administrative problems beyond those contemplated by the original tort system, essentially can be dealt with by existing principles of causation. When we get to cases involving low dose exposure and latent effects, I am not sure our existing conceptions of causation really address the problem. This is an observation which is not just a problem with the tort system, but is going to be a stumbling block for any kind of compensation system which tries to use causal notions as a compensation criteria. That is what makes me leery about some of the proposals for administrative-statutory compensation systems. I see them as just sort of passing the buck on the causation problems from the judicial realm to the administrative realm, where, indeed, it may become even more politicized, as I think anybody who knows anything about the black lung program will attest to.

What are these causation problems? I have been to various conferences that talk about the causation problem in toxic torts, and I hear scientists get up and say the problem is that lawyers don't understand science and judges don't understand science and everybody is misusing science. I hear that concern repeated in the recommendation of the Justice Department report that we must base causation determinations on credible, scientific evidence. The problem is not that lawyers and judges misunderstand science, but that what the scientific and legal worlds mean by causation are two different things: There are two different goals in mind and there is a certain lack of fit between the conceptions of the two systems.

When epidemiologists, for example, talk about causation, they are never going to be pinpointing individualized causes and effects in the way the legal system expects to be able to do. Epidemiology is inherently an aggregate science. It is looking for statistical aggregate effects in the hope that some generalizations can be made about numerical increases in risks. It is not designed to answer the question: Is it more likely than not that this particular defendant's activity caused this particular plaintiff's injury? Moreover, the increase in the use of things like epidemiology by courts in the latent disease context has given an illusion of scientific certainty to these issues that just isn't there. What we are dealing with in some of the latent exposure cases is what has been called transscience, or things that inherently will be uncertain, at least given current states of knowledge and techniques.

Let me use *Agent Orange* and the debate over whether it has a health effect on humans as an example. My interpretation of Judge Weinstein's dismissal of the claims of those plaintiffs who opted out of the class action for failure to adduce sufficient evidence of causation even to get to a jury was that the judge read inconclusive, uncertain, epidemiological results as tantamount to conclusively negative--"no causation at all" results. I am not saying that acknowledging that the epidemiology was simply uncertain would necessarily have changed the outcome, but when this kind of scientific evidence is being used in the courts it is important to keep in mind that a study showing a more positive correlation would not answer the causation question that the law poses. Nor did the uncertain epidemiological studies negatively answer the question that the law poses. The reason that these studies were uncertain and may be so for a long time, which I think the legal system is going to have to confront, is that dose and route of exposure were unverifiable. The kinds of injuries the people were complaining about can be caused by numerous other substances. They were not injuries unique to a particular substance such as mesothelioma or asbestosis or the kinds of cancer caused by DES. This means that if an epidemiological study could control for dose and exposure--could know those factors--it could perhaps suggest whether there was an increase in background risk of certain cancers from exposure to dioxin.

In light of the inability of epidemiological studies to shed light on individual causation, courts should not too readily rush to rely only on epidemiological evidence. A curious move that Judge Weinstein made in dismissing the opt-out cases is that he ruled that only epidemiological evidence was relevant. Judge Weinstein rejected the relevance of data from accidents like the Seveso, Italy, industrial accident. He said that animals are not humans and the doses were different, and in Seveso the doses and exposure were different than in Vietnam. In Seveso there were chloracne cases. Here we have sarcoma or birth defect cases.

Given the purposes of the causal inquiry in the law, maybe those kinds of evidence rejected by Judge Weinstein should be relevant after all. What I see as the purpose of causation in the law is rather than conclusively in a medical way try to answer a question (upon which to formulate further research or make treatment decisions or give preventive medicine), it is to see if there is a plausible connection between one kind of activity and one kind of effect. For policy reasons we may want to make one actor compensate a victim. That is a very different question from the one that science is pursuing. Given the way our tort system looks for a connection and says that community standards should be brought to bear on whether there is sufficient connection to make someone pay, other sorts of evidence besides scientific evidence, or certainly more than just epidemiological evidence, are necessary.

I want to return to the larger question of whether causation should be used as a compensation criteria at all. Let me first say that these problems of uncertainty in science, which make science unable to provide the answers that we wish it could, is going to plague an administrative system as well. If you take the injuries that might flow from leading dump sites and create a statutory compensation system that depends on causation, you are still going to have to try to figure out what and who caused what. We are still going to have the problems of time lag, multiple and possible causes, and uncertain exposure and dose. If we are going to continue to use causation as a compensatory criterion, I am not sure other systems are going to do any better than tort. They may do it less expensively, but I don't think that necessarily means we should eliminate the tort system because of the other search-for-information or morality play aspects that it fulfills.

Why do we want to use causation as a criteria for compensation? Well, certainly if compensation is your only goal, I don't think causation has anything to do with it. If someone has cancer, that creates needs, and why would it matter whether their cancer can be pinpointed to someone's toxic substance or not? If simply taking care of injured people is what we are concerned about, I don't think we need causation. It is usually said we need causation for fairness reasons to answer not the question of who gets compensated, but "who pays." It is also said that we need causation to make deterrence a viable principle. I happen to agree with certain critics of the tort system; for example, Steven Sugarman, who wrote an article recently in the *Berkeley Law Journal,* asked why do we need tort law at all? Tort law never really has accomplished much in the way of positive deterrence. I do think there is evidence, for example, the vaccine cases--that it may have accomplished negative deterrence in the sense that fear of arbitrariness and increasing judgments and lack of insurability may make people stop marketing valuable products.

I am not sure there is much evidence that tort law has led people to market different products or to stop driving or to drive in a safer fashion or to alter the way one walks across the street. The reason people engage in safer, rather than riskier, conduct is out of concern for their own neck or out of some sense of social responsibility--not because they are worried about possibly getting dragged into court and having to pay a tort judgment. If we are concerned about deterrence, standard setting and regulation may be a much saner way to go about it than the very indirect route of the tort system. So, I am not sure that we need causation as a criterion. But, fortunately or unfortunately, questioning whether we need causation as a criterion for a compensatory system leads to the suggestion that some kind of widespread social insurance is the mechanism to have if it's compensation we are concerned about, and to think about combinations of regulatory systems and criminal systems to try to deal with the deterrence concerns. In this country at this time, social insurance proposals are politically infeasible, so I feel a little bit like a fuzzy-headed academic proposing them.

For the time being we are stuck with these causal problems and, like it or not, the tort system is going to be around for a while. How should it better deal with the causal uncertainty problems raised in toxic tort cases? Should judges just say: "I am sorry plaintiffs, but you don't satisfy the very individualized causation proof requirements developed in the last century, so out of court you go." Should they completely abandon the proof of causation requirement which might lead to what could perhaps be overcompensation or would-be social insurance administered by judges instead of by insurance companies or government officials? I want to propose a sort of muddled, in-the-middle alternative, which is that in evaluating the causal issue in something like the *Agent Orange* case, judges must keep in mind that the apparent failure of proof is not the plaintiff's fault.

It is the fault of the nature of the problem and of the substance of science. It is inherent in the injury itself. In other words, it is just something they are going to have to live with and try to deal with rather than saying plaintiff's lawyers didn't dig hard enough or didn't do the right study or something like that. I also think judges are going to have to keep in mind that epidemiological studies are not definitive either way in answering the causation question that the legal system is supposed to answer. Thus, judges should continue to admit other kinds of evidence that may bear on the issue of whether there is a plausible connection, such as clinical toxicological studies or even out of the scientific realm--more practical things that seem to suggest that maybe there is a plausible connection, such as the fact that the plaintiff was exposed to a substance. The plaintiff did not seem to be exposed to other kinds of possible causes. You are probably saying, well, of course, judges must obviously do that. The problem is that in some of these recent cases, particularly the *Agent Orange* case, judges have not been doing that. They are seizing on epidemiology and epidemiological studies as the sole relevant evidence, and relying too heavily on that. Part of what I am pleading for here is a return to the sort of ad hoc approach, only looking for a plausible connection, rather than trying to search for some illusory measure of scientific proof.

PROFESSOR MURPHY: When people talk about the deterrent effect of tort liability it always suggests to me the question: Why is it that today when we are safety conscious, and when we are more interested in quality control, we are looking at models developed in countries like Japan and Sweden which have almost no tort system at all? We are not looking to our own experience nearly so much as we are to theirs and, in their systems, they have developed a product safety record which is much better than ours.

QUESTION: Well, I think you have to look at the system. Go into a factory today, for example, and you will find people who don't even speak English.

PROFESSOR MURPHY: As long as they speak Japanese they are all right.

PROFESSOR FINLEY: I will just make a few comments on what motivated me to make the observation that tort law is a rather indirect and imperfect deterrent mechanism. There has been minimal empirical work trying to assess whether tort law does indeed have a deterrent effect and, if so, what kind of an effect. There needs to be more. Of the few studies that have been done, there was notably a study funded by the Rand Corporation Institute for Civil Justice written by Eads. It suggests that there is very little deterrent effect of tort law itself, and the kinds of effect it may have are perverse ones. The Rand/Eads-authored study went around to a variety of major corporations and did some research and interviewing regarding tort law. What it found was that the part of the company that is set up to deal with tort law and continues to deal with safety and design are kept about as far apart from each other as can be. Information about tort law, tort judgments, and evolving tort standards rarely if ever filters down to the design, planning, or even the marketing departments. The study also found that the tort system is arbitrary and delay ridden. There is a variety of very vague standards from state to state--that often companies tend to treat the tort system as random noise that maybe they had better get some insurance for or put some money aside for. But how can companies possibly take that into account in their design or manufacturing decisions? What one jury says is a safe design another is going to come along and say is a bad design; what one jury says caused something another will say did not. So, if the tort system is a lottery, they might as well take their chances rather than engage in costly restructuring of the way they do business.

This study and some others also suggested that yes, certainly, since the 1960s there has been generally increased concern about safety in the manufacturing and product sectors, but the question that gets raised is whether that is primarily attributable to tort law or to increased societal concern about safety and hazards, and to concerns companies have about their image and the competitive success of their products. Now, the publicity surrounding work like Ralph Nader's study of the Corvair and the initial tort suits may, probably do, help foster those concerns. But I think that doesn't blunt the force of the observation that tort law and the outcomes in the tort system itself are still very imperfect and very indirect, sending often perverse and very indirect deterrence messages to the manufacturers of products.

That leads me to say that if deterrence is important, and if it's really what we are concerned about--is the tort system the most direct and effective way to deter? That was really my point.

QUESTION: As a group of professionals I wonder whether we're addressing the problem as it has an impact on all of the professions, not necessarily the legal profession. We study tort law--I remember Dean Smith saying insurance was the way of spreading the risk. Well, now we've reached the point where we almost have an insurance crisis. I think Mr. Locks would probably admit that when he searches for those defendants with the statute of limitation running only three days hence, he is doing it because he fears that he will be faced with a professional responsibility question. If he fails to turn up that deep pocket during that period, he is afraid that he will spend his time with the balance of his life defending against a malpractice claim which could wipe him and all of his assets out. Whether it's the lawyer in the securities field who can have overwhelming liabilities, or the accountant who can have overwhelming liabilities, the absence of insurance at reasonable cost, has resulted in real social problems today. That is, people of great capability are leaving the professions because of the fear of professional responsibility that is not so much a matter of ultimate liability but the matter only of the defense. If the insurance system is breaking down, then we have to address that problem. I submit that we haven't had any discussion as to the impact on the professional who is facing this problem day by day.

QUESTION: Coming back to the question of deterrence, from your experience does the tort system help encourage companies to avoid unsafe activities and products? In the case of consumer products and industrial products, does the tort system help and encourage a large company to avoid unsafe activities and products? And from the point of view of the insurance company, does the tort system encourage insurance companies to work with their customers to avoid unsafe activities and products? And if not, why not?

MR. MIDDLEBROOK: Sure it does. The issue is one of balance. The insurance companies are going to work as we have always worked with liability insureds to help them make safe products and render safe services up front, because we don't want high exposure and we try to limit that as much as possible. We have engineering labs. We have people who do nothing during every working moment of their day other than to visit sites of potential and actual insureds to help them improve their processes. That's because there is a clear cause and effect in terms of the size of losses. But we do that for first party losses, too. It's not just a tort system that stimulates us to do that. We don't want factories to burn down so that we have to pay large losses there either. So we go around and try to find out what makes them safer. With regard to the whole deterrence argument, I guess we need at least one horror story before we leave.

This is a true story. It involves a ladder manufacturer from my hometown who had found it increasingly difficult to get insurance. He became increasingly angry at my industry because he could not get it. Ladders, for some reason or another, have become a favorite subject for tort liability suits. If you have bought a ladder recently, you will see a lot of stickers on it indicating all the things that can go wrong when you use it--most of which perhaps are common sense. My ladder-manufacturing friend now worries that the next tort suit will be from the fellow who falls off the ladder because he's spending all his time reading the labels going up. But this manufacturer was so angry and so outraged at the conspiratorial nature of the insurance business driving up rates that he got together with several other manufacturers. They went to the Bahamas and formed a ladder insurance company three or four years ago. His reserves or that company's exposures have now gone up by exactly the same rates as ours have, and he is no longer a critic of our industry. He has found somebody else to criticize. So, I think it is just a matter of balance. We have obviously skewed it too much when those kinds of situations can arise--where everybody spends all the time worrying about protection from some creative plaintiff's next liability suit.

MR. KENNEDY: I think the answer to your question is yes by a narrow margin. Obviously, the prospect of compensating for harm provides a motivation to try to minimize the likelihood of the harm and, in my observation, the fact that claims might be asserted--that a liability might be incurred--is something you consider in designing products--certainly in the last two decades. On the other hand, there is the problem of overdeterrence. I think it's very clear that, for example, the withdrawal of Dow/Merrill from the Bendectin market, the withdrawal of Searle from IUDs and, with the fact that we have only one manufacturer of DPTs, you can have overdeterrence.

There is also the random noise problem that Professor Finley was referring to. The wide perception in the engineering and business communities is that the tort litigation system in the United States is absolutely crazy and irresponsible--that almost no matter what you do, you are not necessarily responding the way some jury or court might think you should. As a consequence, there is attention to safety, leaving aside the prospect of compensation. But the attention to safety is not addressed to precise rules in the tort system. I think you would get the same effect from a statutory compensation system. I don't understand the observation of the gentleman earlier that the worker compensation system is not a motivation for safety in the workplace. There are a lot of things wrong with the worker compensation system, but the fact that you are going to have to pay people injured in the workplace doesn't mean that you don't pay attention to what is going on there.

PROFESSOR FINLEY: I wanted to make just one more comment on the deterrence problem, specifically in the context of these toxic exposure latent disease cases. With these cases deterrence models break down, whether in the tort system or in an administrative regulatory system, and it also relates to part of the problem in insurance. One of the commentators said that the whole system of spreading the risk really doesn't work anymore. One reason this is so in the toxic latent disease context is the problem of how can you spread a risk when you are not sure what the risk is? When is it going to manifest itself and to what extent is it going to do so? That is one deterrence problem where you have to know what is unsafe, why it's unsafe, and how to change it. Another problem is from the lag time--the lapse of time. When the risk becomes appreciated it is often far too late. It has been created. What you may be deterring again is new vaccines or new drugs from entering the market. It is hard to tell what you will be deterring when in the 1980s we are assessing whether the use of dioxin-contaminated herbicides in Vietnam twenty years ago has caused cancer.

Another aspect of this is the latency and uncertainty of risk problem and how it relates to deterrence. I think a good way to illustrate the problem is an anecdote related to me by someone involved with regulating the disposal of hazardous wastes. Today's state-of-the-art waste disposal site in full compliance with the requirements of the Resource, Conservation and Recovery Act (RCRA) statute will probably be twenty years from now tomorrow's superfund disaster that we are going to have to clean up. An awful lot of the waste sites that we have to clean up today have wastes in them that were disposed according to what twenty, thirty, or forty years ago we thought were the best, safe, and proper way of disposal. This is a problem, but not necessarily a problem with the tort system. It is a problem with our whole idea of risk and of limitations on our state of knowledge. These problems are going to plague an administrative regulatory system as well as the tort system. It certainly makes it very difficult to insure and to know what you're insuring for.

MR. KENNEDY: I did not want to address a question to Professor Finley, but rather to comment on her observations on causation and the relationship of the causation issue to statutory compensation systems. She may have thought she was disagreeing with me, but I agree with her. I don't think you can have a statutory system that will work where causation is problematic. I think such a system would work only in cases where causation is reliably determinable on a basis which would command a broad scientific consensus. I should have been clearer on that point.

Now, I did want to make another set of observations about causation. I read Judge Weinstein's opinion dismissing the claims of the opt-out plaintiffs in the *Agent Orange* litigation. I read it shortly after it came out and was fascinated, although I confess I haven't looked at it for many months now. There are intriguing observations about expert testimony and the criteria for admissibility of such testimony. I don't envy the attorneys for the plaintiffs who are in the position of trying to persuade the Second Circuit that Judge Weinstein misapplied the Federal Rules of Evidence. Judge Weinstein had apparently immersed himself in the scientific literature; he has an appendix, if I remember rightly, citing massive amounts of it. I read it as saying that one cannot totally exclude the possibility of a connection between exposure to Agent Orange and the health effects alleged by the plaintiff-veterans. But I understood him as also saying that current knowledge simply provides no basis for finding such a connection. It may be that he rationalized the strategy of extracting a settlement in that case on the basis of these two premises; namely, that since you could not totally exclude the possibility of a causal nexus, a settlement applied to funding a medical monitoring mechanism was a pragmatic and fair resolution of the particular and difficult concerns presented in the *Agent Orange* litigation.

Now, although Judge Weinstein's strategy was, within the four corners of that litigation, both pragmatic and innovative, one has to think of the longer-range consequences of the strategy. As I understand it, at least one chemical company defendant was told in London after the settlement: "You have judges in your country who say there is no proof of causation, but you have to pay $180 million to settle the case." We can't insure a system like that. More broadly, and further to what Professor Finley was saying, I don't think the solution in cases of problematic causation is to try to find ways to get judges and juries to resolve them more effectively. We are getting decisions from the courts that the scientific community is saying don't make any sense. I wonder if you can run a rational claims compensation system--whether a statutory system or the conventional tort system--on a basis which is at war with accepted assumptions in the scientific community.

QUESTION: Nobody has said anything about what seems to be a problem with respect to the expectations of the plaintiffs as to what is owed them when they bring suits. We all take risks everyday. When I take the main elevator in the Columbia Law School I may go through the roof or I may go down through the cellar. I know I'm taking a risk. Why should I not have that fact recognized when the recovery is decided upon and take some responsibility for that?

MR. LOCKS: I appreciate that question. I avoided getting into the deterrent discussion of the erratic verdicts and values. But there is a certain deterrent effect to plaintiffs, based upon the erratic decisions that seem to come from juries and judges. There is also a realism among plaintiffs of what is a viable cause of action and what is not. All the evils of deterrence on the manufacturers' and defendants' side we have on our side. Not only do we have them, we have them without adequate funding because most of our plaintiffs, as you know, do not have money and we work on contingent fees. Even though we greedy contingent fee lawyers--a few of us--seem to have accomplished some results that make us fairly affluent, we still are business people and we do not take cases that don't have some viability in them. No, admittedly, what Mr. Middlebrook said is right, there are colleagues of mine and members of the plaintiff bar who do round up cases and advertise and that is the system. But it's not all that bad because it's not all that big. Those fellows can be dealt with and are dealt with, and the system deals with them.

On a massive level, when experienced counsel comes into complicated causal relationships and medical questions, they get resolved. I am not talking about myself, but all I can say is that I was brought into *Agent Orange* five years after it had in fact started. None of the plaintiffs at that point, in all candor, had addressed themselves to trying the case or addressed themselves to causation. We tried in five months to come to the reality of the nuts and bolts of what happened, and it was resolved because of a substantial amount of the uncertainties of winning or losing. That is the system. It probably would not have happened quite the same way if that had been faced five years earlier by the lawyers who got involved in the case. So, I really think that you have to understand--we do truly--that some of us take a good hard look at cases. And we sure are not going to get into cases where ultimate success does not in some way reward our efforts. Therefore, a lot of these cases go by the wayside. But sometimes in the latter situation I guess it keeps magnifying.

PROFESSOR MURPHY: I would just like to say that I very much appreciate our guests being here. I think they have put on a great panel and, if you want us back next year, we will probably have them return to continue the argument. Thank-you all very much.

NEW LIMITATIONS ON DEFENDANT'S RIGHT TO COUNSEL

Moderator:

VIVIAN O. BERGER
Professor of Law, Columbia University

Panelists:

RUDOLPH GIULIANI
U.S. Attorney,
Southern District of New York

GARY NAFTALIS
Partner, Kramer, Levin, Nessen,
Kamin & Frankel

H. RICHARD UVILLER
Professor of Law, Columbia University

PROFESSOR BERGER: We are now concerned primarily with problems that very much affect retained counsel and their clients, not just indigent criminal defendants, like the Scottsborough Boys and Clarence Gideon, who could not even afford to hire counsel.

Pronouncements on counsel and defense representation, at least in my view, have been somewhat less upbeat recently. Within the last few years, the Supreme Court has announced that there is no right to a "meaningful lawyer-client relationship" between lawyer and criminal defendant, and has annunciated doctrine, making it very difficult for defendants to obtain relief if their counsel represented them inadequately. Within the last few days, the Court declined to upset a conviction where, among other things, the police deliberately deceived a lawyer about whether her client, a criminal suspect, would be interrogated that night. Switching our gaze from the citadel to the lower courts and, to the court of public opinion, essentially TV and the newspapers, we are perhaps more likely to receive an image of defense counsel as "mob mouthpiece" than as Clarence Darrow.

Our speakers will focus on some very concrete topics. I suspect there will be fewer matters concerning the Supreme Court and more mundane matters of particular concern to the actors in the criminal justice system. In white collar and generally drug-related cases, I imagine that two very hot areas of discussion will involve subpoenas to defense attorneys, which has become a very big issue nowadays, and statutory forfeiture of attorney's fees in certain cases. So, without further ado, let me give you Mr. Naftalis.

MR. NAFTALIS: It is a pleasure to appear here and speak on a topic of great concern in the criminal justice system: the critical topic of preserving the right to counsel and the adversary system as we have come to know it over the years. There has been what I would consider a sea change in the techniques and tactics employed by federal prosecutors in dealing with criminal defense counsel. Vivian adverted to two of the matters and I want to advert to three of them. One is that criminal defense counsel, as opposed to just plain lawyers, have received grand jury and trial subpoenas falling upon them to divulge information, which even if it is not technically privileged, such as fee information and identity of client, is information that is learned in the course of an attorney-client relationship. They are called upon to testify and the consequence is that they might end up being a witness against the very person whom they are charged to represent. Therefore, they end up being disqualified as counsel.

The second area I would like to speak a little bit about is the area of forfeiture. Under a law called the Comprehensive Forfeiture Act of 1984, prosecutors have sought with some success to forfeit legal fees paid to lawyers in cases brought under the RICO Statute as well as in drug cases; thus, the effect of the successful forfeiture of legal fees, often, if not always, is the deprivation of the right of counsel at all for those defendants. The third matter, which has not really been implemented very much yet, but is on the horizon, is a new law called an amendment to the Currency and Foreign Transactions and Reporting Act. It requires counsel, defense counsel amongst others, to report on pieces of paper called Form 8300s and cash fees from their clients in excess of $10,000. Of course the lawyer is put in the position of actually investigating his clients and creating evidence, which can then be used as the basis to bring a criminal case against someone--say for tax evasion--who may not even have been under investigation in the first place.

Now, these are not issues which are singular in my view to people who represent organized crime defendants, or drug dealers. Indeed, that's not part of my practice, and it seems to me that these are matters that need to be of concern to the bar in general, including the criminal defense bar, as well as the organized bar. Historically, at least, our system of justice has been based upon a balance of forces-- an adversary system of which both sides have counsel--counsel of choice. They go forward zealously, aggressively, and ethically within the rules and before a tribunal, whether it be judge or jury. A result is reached and counsel strives to win. Whether the defendant wins or the government wins in a criminal case, as long as the game is played fairly and the rules are fair, then justice has triumphed. I think there is some kind of slogan to that effect on the wall of the Department of Justice.

It seems to me that the growth of subpoenaing lawyers and turning them into witnesses and the possible forfeiture of their law fees threaten to undermine and upset the delicate balance of forces in our adversary system between the defense and the government. If abused, it creates the possibility of giving prosecutors almost unfettered discretion to have a veto power over counsel in particular criminal cases, and the discretion to determine whether or not in this case a defendant will have counsel of choice or no counsel of choice.

This seems to me not sound public policy. It is not a price which ought to be or which is worth paying for some marginal improvement in the enforcement of the criminal laws. Indeed, some prosecutors have gone on public record (obviously these are the aberrant ones) and explicitly stated that such rules are very good, because criminal defense lawyers don't have a useful role to play in the criminal justice system. In a recent newspaper interview, the United States Attorney for the Southern District of California, not the Southern District of New York, expressed his belief, and I am quoting: "Defense lawyers are not doin' any good for society because, unlike prosecutors, they have no obligation to make sure the guilty are convicted." I certainly don't quarrel with the second part of the quote: "Lawyers that are in private practice are there to make money. They are not altruistic; they are not there generally to do any good for society. If they wanted to do that, they would be prosecutors doing good for society."

Some people who have antiquated views might think that a vigorous, competent, ethical, high-minded, and zealous defense bar does no good for society. Indeed, there are instances where I was privileged recently to get a reversal in a case in the Second Circuit Court of Appeals involving a lawsuit which should not have been brought. It involved a misuse of the federal securities laws, again by a different prosecutor's office. A man was wrongly convicted, who I actually believed was innocent, and the Second Circuit said that he was innocent. I think that was as good for society in terms of getting the right result in that case, as it would be convicting a guilty person in another case.

The philosophy of that abhorrent United States attorney from the West Coast has been translated into practice. A Professor William Genego of the faculty of the University of Southern California Law School has done some empirical work in which he polled members of a defense organization called the National Association of Criminal Defense Lawyers. He got a fairly high response rate in his survey. It is the subject of a paper to be published soon, and he said that some 66 percent of the respondents reported that they had been the subject of one or more of the following things: grand jury subpoenas, IRS summonses, undisclosed informants in lawyers' offices, attempted forfeiture of legal fees, and attempted disqualification of counsel. Genego also stated that his study showed that these practices dramatically increased in the last thirty months and, indeed, were almost unknown prior to 1980. The survey showed that the incident of these subpoenas and forfeiture and other like practices were highest amongst those who practiced either in complicated white-collar cases or drug cases. They were the most experienced and the highest earners in the defense bar. Having not received such a subpoena, I was somewhat insulted after reading the results of that survey.

Let's talk a little bit about the problems in two of the areas at least--subpoenas to lawyers--why are they being done and why in my view they should not be done. Should there be only certain limitations and restraints? The reason is primarily to get fee information. That is why lawyers are paid by the clients. That is historically, save for certain exceptions, a nonprivileged area. It is being done for two purposes. One, to use the fee information as a basis for forfeiting the legal fee later. Secondly, to use as an element of substantive proof in RICO cases, continuing criminal enterprise cases, or tax evasion cases. I can't quarrel that such evidence would be relevant. It would not be relevant in those kinds of cases, but I would suggest as a matter of public policy that that is not a desirable technique.

First of all, it chills the attorney-client relationship. That relationship all of us know is one based upon trust and confidence. Clients go into lawyers' offices and they expect what they say to be secret. Clients do not make fine distinctions between what they say in sentence one and what they say in sentence two. They don't expect their lawyers to be testifying before grand juries behind closed doors about what they have told them. Obviously, that has an inhibiting effect on what clients say to lawyers then and later. If you want to represent clients effectively, you must be sure they tell you the full truth--good, bad, and indifferent. Secondly, subpoenaing lawyers puts them in a position of conflict. Defense lawyers don't just have one case; they have a lot of cases usually. Unless one is a bull in a china shop, one likes to have a decent working relationship--a sense of credibility--with the prosecutor's office, and that does put conscious and subconscious pressure on certain lawyers to cooperate, I think, with inquiries where maybe they should not. Thirdly, it diverts the attention and energy of the lawyer from the true task. The true task of the defense lawyer is representing the client and exercising energy on behalf of the client. Instead, if he or she receives a subpoena, the energy or attention has to be diverted in dealing with that subpoena, contesting it, perhaps hiring counsel to go out and litigate it, and, therefore, the attention is being diverted away from what the real business ought to be. Fourthly, subpoenas to lawyers deter advocacy.

Sometimes counsel has to worry about being too aggressive, too nasty, too obnoxious--am I going to set myself up for some assistant U.S. attorney to put a subpoena on me? That may deter zealous, aggressive, and proper advocacy. Finally, what I consider bad about subpoenaing lawyers is that it creates the possibility in the wrong hands of manipulating the choice of counsel and having them disqualified. Under the ethical rules, which I am sure Dick Uviller will talk about, and in which he is much more conversant than I, counsel may not continue to represent a client if he or she will be a witness against that client and the testimony is prejudicial. By subpoenaing counsel for information, making them witnesses to disqualify counsel, prosecutors have the ability to exercise a veto power over who shall or who shall not represent someone in a particular case.

Now, this kind of problem is not as bad in a large urban area like New York where there is a very healthy and extensive defense bar, but these kinds of rules apply everywhere. In smaller communities you don't necessarily have that many criminal defense lawyers. In one case in New Hampshire, where trial subpoenas were served in the middle of the night, a defense counsel lived on some little road in the middle of nowhere. Those subpoenas were quashed on the grounds that it was harassment of counsel. (You know there aren't that many criminal defense lawyers in New Hampshire. If you go out and disqualify five of them, you really aren't going to have that many left.) Therefore, prosecutors really do have the ability to determine who is in and who is out. What are the remedies? Well, sad to say, the second circuit in the so-called Slotnick case a couple of months back decided that the Fifth and Sixth Amendments do not protect attorneys in such a situation. They do not require any prior judicial approval or any showings before an attorney may be subpoenaed. However, I don't think that's the end of the matter because there is a need for restraint. The organized bar, the American Bar Association, the New York State Bar Association, and the Association of the Bar of the City of New York have all called for prior judicial approval before subpoenas are issued to lawyers.

Obviously, these are conservative organizations of the legal establishment--not lobbyists for the mob or organized crime. In Massachusetts, the United States attorney there issued in the last year some fifty subpoenas for lawyers. I didn't even know there were fifty criminal defense lawyers in Boston. This led the Supreme Judicial Court of Massachusetts to adopt a disciplinary rule that it is unethical behavior to subpoena lawyers to testify about their clients' matters without prior judicial approval. Florida is in the process of considering a similar rule. In the teeth of this, the Department of Justice has promulgated guidelines which I am sure Rudy Giuliani will speak about, and the United States attorney's office here has guidelines, too. I suggest that is not enough.

These guidelines say that they are not enforceable in court; they do not create any legal rights and, if we are going to create rules, they ought to be rules enforced by the court. The violation of those rules should give some remedy. It seems to me that there is no good reason why there shouldn't be prior judicial approval of the issuance of a subpoena to a lawyer. I don't think that prosecutors could have much trouble in an *ex parte* proceeding if they have a truly good case of convincing a judge that their grand jury subpoena ought to issue and, if not, then that subpoena probably ought not to issue. In order for those subpoenas to issue, there should be at least three things about them: that the evidence is really essential--not cumulative. And, that there is no feasible alternative--that is, you have exhausted any realistic prospect of getting it elsewhere. I would go further in the postindictment context. Once you have an indictment in place, it means that you've done your investigation. You've had your grand jury work, you've had your investigative agencies, whether it be the FBI, the SEC, or whatever, and you should be ready to go to trial. Indeed, the Speedy Trial Act mandates that you are supposed to go to trial within a very short period of time. Under those circumstances, it ought to be a very extraordinary event if, after the indictment is in place, the government should be allowed to subpoena the trial counsel for the man or woman under the indictment who is getting ready to face that charge.

Forfeiture is closely related to the subpoena topic. As I said before, the government has the right to forfeit assets in RICO cases. Now RICO cases are not just all organized crime cases. RICO is a law that one wag said was passed for the purpose of protecting businessmen against gangsters, and it has had the effect of making businessmen gangsters. I got something in the mail called the *RICO Law Report*. It came recently and there was a little headline that said: "Mickey Mouse, a Racketeer." It turned out that Walt Disney was being sued civilly for civil RICO in some claim or other. Now RICO, of course, can be charged criminally or civilly. There are a whole variety of matters that go well beyond the Mafia. In the public corruption cases that Rudy Giuliani's office just brought, there have been RICO charges. All kinds of white-collar cases can be made into RICO cases on the basis of two mail frauds.

The possibility of forfeiting someone's legal fees in this case is a penalty which is too great for our system to bear. The RICO forfeiture penalties were put in for a good reason. They were designed to prevent defendants from retaining the fruits of their crimes and, in that regard, they were designed to prevent them from retaining them, both directly and indirectly; that is to say, hiding it themselves or engaging in a sham or bogus transfer where it is put in an anonymous name or front's name. It can be some phony corporation and hidden. It is perfectly appropriate to go after those sham and bogus transfers, and if an attorney acts in a way to facilitate that kind of enterprise or acts like a criminal, then I have no sympathy. I think that with any money sent to attorneys for the purposes of any true money laundering or true hiding of assets, one ought to be able to go after them, but that is a good deal different from going after the payment of legitimate legal fees to a lawyer for the representation of a defendant in a criminal case. It is no different than going after the payment of tuition to Columbia for a racketeer's son or for the medical services rendered by a physician. If this is successful, it would eventually take the adversary out of the adversary process and deprive individuals of counsel at all. I think this is wrong.

First, it conflicts with the presumption of innocence. Essentially, you have the possibility of the penalty before conviction. As the queen said, sentence first, verdict afterwards. Some people may even be innocent and still be deprived of counsel. Secondly, it puts attorneys in a kind of conflict situation they ought not to be in. An attorney ought to be thinking of the client's welfare--not about payment. Attorneys should not have hanging over their heads, the notion that "gee, if I adopt this tactical decision, as opposed to that tactical decision, it enhances the possibility of me getting a fee as opposed to not getting a fee."

People should not go to trial on behalf of their clients only to avoid a plea of guilty, which may result in forfeiture of a legal fee. Similarly, and there is some documentation of this in Professor Genego's study, there are instances of lawyers who entered into plea bargains without a forfeiture element of legal fees, and they were told that the alternative was to enter into a plea bargain. They went to trial and the government ought to have asked for forfeiture of legal fees. That is not the kind of conflict situation you want lawyers to be in. That is not the kind of advocacy our system wants. You do not want lawyers in the situation where they are trying criminal cases on a contingency. That violates the ethical rules. The fact is that some people will be deprived of counsel altogether. Many lawyers or most lawyers are not going to take cases if they are subject to forfeiture. And yet, you have the kind of anomalous situation of where can this person get counsel? Can a person really fill out a criminal justice act form saying he or she has no assets truthfully, when the person really does have assets? At the same time, a lawyer may not want to touch the case because there may be no payment for it. The American Bar Association and the City Bar have come out against forfeiture of bona fide legal fees. Chief Judge Motley and Judge Leval have written opinions where they have struck down attempts either to restrain payment of legal fees or to restrain the forfeiture of legal fees. I think that is the healthy way and that fighting crime is valid. The current U.S. Attorney of the Southern District of New York has done a wonderful job in fighting crime. What we need though is a balance for our adversary system where defendants' rights to counsel are preserved at the same time.

I will just close with a reference to the study of Professor Genego's. His study showed that some of these practices I mentioned earlier have, in fact, inhibited vigorous defense advocacy. Thirty-one percent of the people who responded to the survey believed that their action in criminal cases has been affected by a fear that somehow the government would retaliate. Whether that fear is justified, or unjustified, why should lawyers have that kind of fear? Fourteen percent of the people in the survey stated that they declined representation because they feared their fees would be forfeited. Twenty-nine attorneys said they are taking fewer criminal cases as a consequence. Sixteen lawyers responded that they have decided to end their federal criminal practices. They did not want to be subpoenaed and risk possible damage to their reputations.

In this area, we have a vigorous criminal defense bar. Many of the people are former assistant U.S. attorneys from my generation or so, and I think they practice at a high level. It is not in the public interest to deter intelligent, aggressive, and experienced people from entering the world of criminal defense and set a barrier such as forfeiture of legal fees. That would drive them into other areas and perhaps leave the criminal defense area to people who were more unscrupulous--who were willing to take cash fees under the table and not tell anybody. As for them, none of these rules really matter. Thank-you.

MR. GIULIANI: If occasionally prosecutors have made some silly statements about defense attorneys, it is incredible the number of hysterical statements made by defense attorneys about subpoena, litigation, and also seizure of attorney fees. In fact, from the very beginning, the reaction to this by the defense bar and the bar in general has been hysterical, rather than rational and intelligent. They misconceive and misstate constantly what the legislation provides and what the guidelines of the Justice Department are. They also give the impression that prosecutors can just subpoena anyone they want and seize legal fees without it ever being tested in court. We can move into lawyers' offices and take millions of dollars out of their offices, because that is basically the kind of fees we are talking about. We can deprive them of those fees without due process, without decisions in court, without the applications of legal standards, and without the ability of these lawyers to litigate, litigate, and litigate all over again the whole propriety of what is being done. The things that we will talk about are not things that exist in the sole discretion of the prosecutor or in the unfettered discretion of the prosecutor. If they did, that would be a terrible thing and it would be a terrible mistake. Every single thing that we are talking about are issues that get determined in the court. There is a reason for that.

Now I wonder where the American Bar Association and Professor Genego were? I wonder where he was, studying the incidence of lawyers taking cash fees and not paying taxes on those fees? I wonder where the American Bar Association and Professor Genego were and what recommendations they made about lawyers who act as house counsel to organized crime families, to drug importation groups who aid and abet those groups in their ability to bring millions and millions of dollars worth of heroin and cocaine into our cities. This has been going on for twenty or thirty years. I don't remember a solid recommendation from the American Bar Association about the social reality that has to be dealt with, and I don't remember any studies from Professor Genego about it. That is an issue we ignore and do not look at. There is a balance that is necessary here. There is a simple reality that lawyers have to recognize--that lawyers violate the law in serious ways at a level at least equal to others in society. We have a fair percentage of lawyers who violate the law in a serious manner; by no means all lawyers, by no means some very large percentage of lawyers, but also by no means just one or two bad apples.

In fact, there is a problem and there has been a problem over several decades now of lawyers who have demeaned and reduced the public reputation of the legal profession and the American Bar Association. What have other bar associations and Professor Genegos done about that? This is why the United States Congress had to act, because lawyers did not discipline themselves and did not create standards to remove this problem from the legal profession. The legislation passed that we have been talking about is not novel; it does not offend any of the constitutional decisions that, at least, relate to subpoenas of attorneys. Attorney fee information has never been covered by the attorney-client privilege. In fact, attorneys now want to challenge subpoenas on the grounds that a new Sixth Amendment privilege, right, or an extension of that privilege or right should be made, because the subpoenas are oppressive and interfere with the right to counsel. In essence, what they are really asking for is an extension of the present law. The legislation passed by Congress and the legislation in which the Justice Department relies on subpoenaing attorneys is all within well-established precedent insofar as the attorney-client privilege is concerned.

Now let me tell you what the Justice Department has done to try to lessen areas of possible conflict, because the end result here has to be a balance. Attorneys cannot be immune from subpoenas. They are not entitled to be immune from subpoenas; presidents of the United States are not entitled to be immune from subpoenas. Easily, the areas of knowledge and information that they obtain are as sensitive if not more sensitive than defense attorneys or any attorney. There has to be a balance that is worked out. The same thing is true about seizure of attorney's fees in RICO cases. Obviously, the government should not be able to seize all attorneys' fees and all RICO cases, just because someone is convicted of RICO. That is the impression one gets if you listen to the defense bar talk about this hysterically. In fact, the government can only seize, under the RICO statute, an attorney's fees after a trial, after a conviction, and after a specific hearing. The government has to show that the lawyer had reason to believe that the fees were "dirty money"; that the money was drug money, extortion money, or money that came from the RICO transaction established beyond a reasonable doubt.

Over and above that standard, the Justice Department has regulations which require more proof than that. It requires proof, not only that the attorney had reason to know, which might be too general a standard, but that in fact the attorney knew what was being received was "dirty money." That is a very difficult standard to meet. It may even be in some cases that some prosecutors believe it's an impractical standard, but it is one that isolates forfeiture in situations where an attorney is engaged in conduct among the most egregious, possibly even criminal, but certainly a justifiable basis for seizing a fee. It does not occur based on the unfettered discretion of the prosecutor. The prosecutor has to obtain first a conviction in a court beyond a reasonable doubt, proving the existence of the RICO enterprise. Then there has to be a hearing before the court in which the prosecutor has to satisfy them that the attorney took the money knowing that this was the proceeds of a drug transaction, an extortion transaction, or a major fraud transaction. You should also understand that unlike civil RICO, which was mentioned, criminal RICO is a very, very different animal.

Before I can indict someone or any U.S. attorney can ask for an indictment under the RICO statute, I have to obtain approval from the Department of Justice. There are very specific requirements that RICO only be used in cases of substance; that we cannot use RICO in a two-predicate mail fraud case, is a *de minimus* case. We have to be able to establish that it is a very substantial fraud in the hundreds of thousands or millions of dollars before the Justice Department will approve a RICO prosecution. There are internal guidelines and restrictions on the way the RICO statute can be applied in the first instance, and there are internal restrictions and guidelines on the situations in which attorneys will be subject to forfeiture. The situations have to be ones where we have proof that the attorney knew that the money being gotten was, in fact, money from the illegal transaction. This issue became very heated last year. When I testified before the Bar Association, I predicted there would be only rare instances in which the government would seek seizure of attorney's fees, and there would possibly be more, but still relatively few instances in which the United States government would subpoena an attorney for fee information.

In my office, when this legislation was first enacted, we instituted a procedure whereby, whenever an assistant U.S. attorney wants to subpoena a lawyer, under any circumstances, including where an attorney was a witness to a crime or a subject of a criminal investigation, we require that the assistant U.S. attorney obtain the approval of the U.S. attorney. We keep a file on that. The Justice Department has now made it a written regulation that one has to get the permission of the assistant attorney general in charge of the criminal division before you can subpoena an attorney for any reason, whether it is fee information or what would be old-fashioned reasons for subpoenaing an attorney, just like anyone else.

During that period of time, I believe we have had no more than four or five subpoenas in a year for fee information. They are very rarely used—only with a great deal of discretion, a great deal of care, and with very substantial internal controls. We only approve a subpoena to an attorney in a situation where we are satisfied ourselves and are not seeking information that is covered by the attorney-client privilege. That is what we do internally, but you and the public are not subjected to a decision based on our arbitrary decision. If an attorney disputes the question of whether or not we are seeking information that is covered by the privilege, the attorney can make a motion to quash the subpoena. The attorneys that obtain such subpoenas know how to do it. These are not unschooled, shy, or naive people, who are just going to get the subpoena from the government. It is not going to just slip their minds that maybe this is reaching information that is covered by the privilege. These are people who litigate for a living. If we make a mistake in our internal determination, or if the attorney is not satisfied with our internal determination, he or she can make something which I think all of these people know how to do in front of a judge. He or she is wrong. This information will violate constitutional principles, statutory principles, or some articulated law that can be applied by the court. We have litigated several of those, and that is the way these decisions are made: in a court, not by the prosecutor.

The simple fact is that forfeiture legislation and occasional subpoenas to attorneys are necessary because of the conduct of attorneys. Whenever I say this, that is precisely what the defense lawyers take away from it: that I am saying they are all involved in illegal or unethical behavior with organized criminals and with drug defendants. They are not by any means. But by the same token, please do not think it is just an occasional, single, or isolated instance. It is more than that and it is something that has to be resolved in court. There has to be a balance struck between the legitimate interest of the government--in investigating and curtailing the activities of these lawyers who are acting illegally and unethically--and the rights of lawyers and clients to obtain the full and complete representation of their clients.

If Congress had passed a law that said I could just seize attorneys' fees any time I wanted when I decided that there was a racketeering enterprise, then I could understand the hysterical reaction of the defense bar. If I have to prove to a judge that a forfeiture will only take place where a United States judge is convinced that a defense lawyer knew that the money was stolen property--the defrauded cash, the drug money, the extortion money, the contract murder money--then, if that's the case, it seems to me that that is a reasonable balance between two very important issues: between the right to counsel and the problem that we have some lawyers engaging in criminal activities with their clients, or getting so close that it is appropriate to treat them the way you would treat anyone else in a forfeiture situation. Those decisions are made ultimately by the United States court at the district court level with the right to appeal to the circuit and to the Supreme Court. It seems to me that that balance has been worked out about as effectively as we know how in the United States. The way we work out balances in other kinds of problems we have to face.

The difference here is, in my view, that the bar associations, particularly with their recommendations--the Bar Association of Massachusetts--and some of the others are really trying to step well beyond their roles as bar associations. Bar associations should not be legislating whether or not United States attorneys and prosecutors should have to seek prior judicial permission in order to subpoena. That is a governmental function. That is something that legislatures should be determining, as a matter of law, and courts should be interpreting or determining as a matter of law--not bar associations. Bar associations have moved over into a whole new realm as quasi-legislatures and, as trade associations, trying to obtain advantages for themselves in earning a living much the same way as other trade associations attempt to put restrictions in order to enhance their ability to earn a living. I think ultimately it will be very, very harmful to the public image and the reality of bar associations. Thank-you.

PROFESSOR UVILLER: Professor Berger, fellow panelists, and guests, until recently, I was ignorant but clearheaded on this matter. Now thanks to the inestimable assistance of two students and one colleague, I am much better informed, but alas somewhat confused. The problem is, of course, the discouragement and distraction of counsel, whose fee may be riding on the outcome of the case or may be called upon as a witness, against his or her client. Now, let me announce my conclusion on this problem. (Here I pause to say do not be alarmed to find that an academic actually reaches conclusions on some problems.)

My position, tentative as it is and informed by my recent education, will be that in a limited set of circumstances the debilitation of private counsel is inescapable, but that the resulting situation is not irremediable. Now uncertain as how to begin to reach that conclusion, I decided to take a daring approach and proceed from principle. First, regarding the matter of fee forfeiture, it seems to me that there is nothing wrong, either as a matter of constitutional law or from a moral standpoint, with a due processed forfeiture of the interest in an illegal enterprise, illegally acquired interest in a legal enterprise, or the profits and proceeds of crime. In fact, concerning proceeds, along with instrumentalities, the idea of forfeiture goes back into the veiled myths of history, at least as long ago as the word "deodand" suggests.

The corollary of the principle is that such proceeds, interest, or profit may be recovered from the hands of any bad faith holder, including the bad faith holder for value. That being the principle, then the issue is: Is there any good reason to exempt the lawyer's fee from the operation of that precept? Now, the stated reasons are two basically: The first being that a private counsel may be conflicted out of the case, meaning required to step down and relinquish representation by reason of conflict. This is said unreasonably to interfere with the defendant's constitutionally protected right to counsel or, as it is frequently put, the right to counsel of choice. Ultimately, if enough lawyers in New Hampshire or elsewhere are conflicted out of the case for the same reason, it will deprive the defendant of representation altogether, and the legal assistance guaranteed the defendant by the Sixth Amendment of the Constitution will be lost. The second of the arguments for exemption from the principle is that even if not conflicted out of the case by a court order, lawyers tend to shun clients whose fees may be forfeited. That is to say, there is a voluntary relinquishment (or I should say a voluntary loss) of the availability of counsel's assistance by reason of the prospect of surrender of the fee.

Let's look at these reasons a bit more closely. Can counsel be conflicted out on the prosecutor's subpoena, however well-founded and carefully circumscribed the prosecutor's exercise of discretion may be? Well, yes, I think the answer to that is: In a particular set of circumstances, there may be an inescapable or unavoidable conflict. Those circumstances I think are these: where an asset is alleged in the indictment as an interest in an illegal enterprise, or the proceeds therefrom, and where the attorney's fee has been paid in the same specie. Now, in most of the cases so far, lawyers' fees were paid in value other than currency, such as an airplane or an equitable interest in some business that was said to be the proceeds or interest in the illegal enterprise and declared forfeit. If the lawyer is paid in the same specie as the asset alleged in the forfeiture count of the RICO indictment, then, of course, the second condition is met. However, where the asset alleged is cash, and the lawyer's fee has been paid in cash, I think the issue is more complex and more difficult.

First of all, there is the problem of tracing the cash. If the defendant in the case has some cash assets which are not claimed to be the proceeds or interest in the illegal enterprise, and the defendant uses that cash fund to pay the lawyer's fee, then, of course, the lawyer's fee is not forfeit. It is a little hard to tell which cash out of a multiple account, some of which is alleged to be proceeds of crime, was the cash used for the attorney's services. Those cash cases are hard to begin with. It seems to me that there might be at least a partial protection for the attorney's fee by the adoption of the rule (which I don't think is the rule as yet)--a rule to the effect that where the asset alleged in the count of the indictment is said to be cash, that that cash is fundible in the hands of the defendant. The asset must be forfeited or collected from the defendant first-- up to the full amount if possible--that is, the full amount found by the jury in the verdict of conviction.

So, if the attorney is representing a defendant, whose own untainted liquid assets amount to or exceed the alleged proceeds of crime, then at least a portion of the attorney's cash fee would be secure. But even in the circumstances in which these conditions are met, and the attorney's fee rides with the verdict, is the conflict avoidable? Frequently the claim is made, and I suppose with some reason, that an attorney, who has a stake in the outcome and whose fee may be forfeited with the loss of the case, is disqualified by reason of conflict of interest to represent the defendant. I have always been slightly confused by that rule. If the attorney's stake in the outcome is precisely the stake of his client, to wit they both want to win, it is difficult for me to see any real conflict of interest between them any more than in any other contingency case in which the energies and efforts of the lawyer will be completely devoted to the interest of the client. It may be even to a greater extent because the attorney shares that interest in the outcome.

But, of course, the problem with these RICO prosecutions is that there are at least two counts, one of which is a substantive count, alleging the participation of the defendant in this racketeer-influenced and corrupt enterprise. The other is a count alleging proceeds or interest from one's participation. It is thought that the attorney may pay more attention to the verdict on the second of those counts than on the first and, to some extent, the attorney may sacrifice the interest of the client on the substantive count. Well, that seems quite problematic to me. I just don't imagine lawyers so dividing their efforts in a case, but in any event, a remedy is possible. We do not have it at the moment, but we certainly could have it. I don't think it would be any great hardship to bifurcate the trial, separating the substantive count from the forfeiture count, and thus assuring the attorney's complete devotion to the client's interest on the substantive count.

There is often a more serious (and less frequently noted) conflict where an attorney undertakes the representation of a defendant in a RICO case containing a forfeiture count. And that is the matter of plea bargaining. Insofar as the United States attorney's office can offer not to pursue the forfeiture count in exchange for a guilty plea to the substantive count, the attorney, whose fee depends upon nonpursuit of the forfeiture count, may be inclined to become an *ex officio* assistant to the United States attorney. The attorney may attempt to persuade the client to plead guilty to the substantive count in order to obtain the assurance that the forfeiture will not be executed against the fee. Now there is no remedy that I can think of for that. Any effort legislatively to take the forfeiture count off the bargaining table so that this kind of trading of interests cannot take place will not work. It's just too important to obtain the disposition of cases to deprive the United States attorney of the option of nonpursuit or nonprosecution of the forfeiture count against the defendant himself. Thus, insofar as plea bargaining remains a very important means for the fair disposition of these cases (as with every other criminal case), it is unrealistic to try to alter artificially those rare and relatively infrequent cases in which the conditions I indicated are all met. So much for fee forfeiture.

Now let's look to the subpoena of the lawyer as a witness. I am informed that the trial subpoenas are as yet more a threat than a reality. Most of the subpoenas that we are talking about are grand jury or investigative subpoenas. In any case, response to a subpoena for relevant and unprivileged evidence is a recognized obligation of lawyers as well as for every other citizen. That is, the ancient maxim that the fact finder, the judicial process, and the grand jury is entitled to every person's evidence if relevant and unprivileged, is undiminished in our jurisprudence. Now given the floating and expansive elements of the crime known affectionately as RICO (and even in those more conventional and older predecessors the frauds by mail and wire), the conspiracy prosecutions, for example, relevance of the information sought regarding fee can hardly be doubted. That leaves the matter of privilege in which the lines are somewhat less clear. We have heard it said today, and I am sure you are all familiar with the axiom that fees, who pays them, how large, and for what, are not privileged. Well, that's a little bit overstated. There are cases in which the fee information was regarded as within the attorney-client privilege, but I am not about to digress into that thicket.

Is there any good reason to exempt the lawyer from the testimonial obligation of subpoena? Well, in one of those extraordinarily rare events in the CA 2, known as *en banc*, the question answered is: No. Are they wrong? Is there any special privilege? Well, this is worth a little bit of thought. There has been some mention made of local efforts to try our ploy. There have been some pathetic efforts by the Massachusetts Bar in the first instance, followed by in one form or another our own, the Florida Bar, and probably others to try to get around the obligation of subpoena by a rule of professional conduct applicable to federal prosecutors. Well, nobody has yet told you, but I am sure you already know that the District Court in the First Circuit, considering the Massachusetts rule, has held that there is nothing inconsistent between the rule of ethics requiring prior approval and the right to counsel.

The reason I say that these efforts are pathetic is because the rule proposed and, I guess, adopted by the Supreme Judicial Court in Massachusetts, is totally empty of any significance. It doesn't even set standards. If the CA 2 is right, there is not even a "relevance" or "necessity" standard. The irony is that if the ethical rule--if the state rule of professional responsibility--is so innocuous that it escapes the supremacy clause when applied to federal prosecutors, then it is utterly worthless for the purpose. It is too mild to serve as any kind of check on the discretionary use of subpoenas by the government.

Does that subpoena disqualify the lawyer by reason of conflict? Well, as to a trial subpoena, I should think the answer is clear; I can't imagine a lawyer representing a client and appearing at the trial on the same case on the witness stand, for any purpose, against the client. In the grand jury, it seems to me, the matter is not so clear. While it may chill, it may discourage, and it may sour the relationship of confidence between the client and the attorney for the attorney to testify in a grand jury, certainly the giving of unprivileged information is not necessarily a disqualification.

What is the remedy? I say the conflict is inescapable either by reason of the forfeiture or by reason of the subpoena. Why do I say that it is not hopeless? Well, what we need to do is to broaden the concept of need (which is a requirement for the assignment of counsel) from economic need to need in general. Wherever a defendant is unable to obtain counsel of choice, simply assign counsel who will provide effective representation. The position I wanted to take here was that the Sixth Amendment of the Constitution accords no right to counsel of choice period. But my good advisor, who is watching me suspiciously at the moment, has persuaded me that this would be a very unlawyerlike position to take, since I don't need to go that far. Therefore, with some reluctance, I give up. I had this great rationale for the position which was that no court would tolerate a differential application of the Sixth Amendment right to counsel, according to the financial condition of the client. Since the indigent have no right to counsel of choice, those who are better off should have no greater right under the Sixth Amendment. But don't be nervous, I do not take that position here. The only position I need to take is that the right to counsel of choice accorded by the Sixth Amendment (such as it is or whatever it may be) is not absolute. And that, of course, is well established.

Indeed, not only is the "right" less than absolute, but the standard upon which it may be lost is relatively light. All that is needed is the term constitutionalists recognize--a "rational basis" for the deprivation. A defendant may not be deprived of effective assistance of counsel under any circumstances, but the choice of counsel may be lost on virtually any reason. If a judge has a fairly good reason to deny an adjournment, for example, a defendant may have to settle for counsel of his second choice. Certainly, the obligations, the principles that I have mentioned--the obligation to give evidence-- and the obligations to surrender the proceeds of crime, constitute a substantial basis for the loss of primary choice in the right to counsel of choice.

PROFESSOR BERGER: Thank-you very much.

RECEPTION AND LUNCHEON REMARKS
Low Memorial Library

Dais Guests:

HON. RENA K. UVILLER,
Alumni Chair, Presiding

DEAN BARBARA ARONSTEIN BLACK
Remarks

HON. FELICE K. SHEA,
Outgoing President

HON. BENJAMIN KAPLAN '33,
Medal for Excellence Recipient

PHILIP A. LACOVARA,
Incoming President

HON. JAMES D. HOPKINS '33,
Medal for Excellence Recipient

PROFESSOR WALTER WERNER,
Faculty Chair

JUDGE UVILLER: Judge Hopkins, Judge Kaplan, and guests, on behalf of the Alumni Association, I welcome you all to the twenty-seventh Columbia Law School Symposium. We have had a richly textured morning and look forward to an equally stimulating afternoon with Abe Sofaer. Permit me now to take just a few moments to express gratitude on behalf of the Alumni Association to those whose efforts have shaped this day: to the participants of each of this morning's three panels for their thoughtful and provocative presentations and exchanges; to the members of the Symposium Committee, who have provided a continuing source of suggested topics for this annual event, keeping us in touch with the concerns and interests of our alumni. Also, our thanks to Dean Arthur Kimball and to Stephanie Straffi, who as Executive Director of the Alumni Association, and Alumni Relations Officer, respectively, have coordinated this event. My especial and deeply felt gratitude to the person most responsible for the intellectual vitality of this Symposium, the breadth of whose interests and whose graceful command of his colleagues' respect and devotion were responsible for today's assemblage of panelists: my cochair for this event, Adolf A. Berle Professor of Law Emeritus, Walter Werner. Thank-you, Walter.

It has been a true pleasure to work with Walter on this, and I am told by Arthur Kimball that he has been responsible for this event under three successive deans in three successive years. That is no instability reflected upon the Columbia Law School, but certainly a vote for the stability provided by Walter Werner. Really, my deep gratitude to you. I would also like to acknowledge the presence, which we are all honored by, of prior recipients of the Medal for Excellence. They are with us today at this luncheon: Honorable Stanley Fuld, Professor

Walter Gellhorn, Professor Herbert Wechsler, Honorable Charles Breitel, Ms. Harriet Pilpel, Professor Louis Henkin, Honorable Oscar H. Davis, and Professor Willis Reese.

Before our brief program begins, may I remind you that Abe Sofaer will deliver the Sulzbacher Memorial Lecture on "Terrorism and the Law" immediately following lunch. It will be held in the Proskauer Auditorium on the ground floor of the Law School and will be followed by coffee and refreshments. At 4:00 p.m. do not miss the student musical. It will contain its usual dose of irreverence and talent and will do its best to both amuse and antagonize in various proportions. I am sure you'll all be delighted by it, however. Finally, on a personal note: As a Law School student of the sixties, and one to whom the frayed adjective "disaffected" surely applied, I am somewhat bemused to find myself here today as cochair of this event. In that decade of the sixties, the Columbia Law School, notwithstanding its many other virtues, was not a particularly happy place for a woman to study law. And so it was against all odds that I would, with such pride in Columbia today, be here to welcome you all. My path, however, is not solely a personal one, for Columbia Law School has changed. Building on the excellence of its tradition, it has broadened and invigorated itself to become the most stimulating and exciting Law School in this country, and I hope you all share that view.

It is a Law School deeply committed, not only to traditional studies, but to the role of law in a changing world of changing values, as I think our morning panels reflected. Barbara Aronstein Black has been selected to lead Columbia Law School because of the excellence of her mind and character. And yet it would be a disservice to the Law School faculty, who unanimously nominated her, not to express special pride in their evolving sensibilities and their wisdom in recognizing Barbara's excellence in choosing the first woman in the long history of this institution. It is a great honor for me to give you our new Dean, Barbara Aronstein Black.

DEAN BLACK: Thank-you very much. Honored guests, alumni, colleagues, and friends, this is a great day for Columbia Law School. Today is the day each year when we pull out all the stops --when alumni and faculty pool their talents and do what they do best--talk. We talk about matters of great significance indeed, and then, over the drinks, perhaps a few of not such great significance. This year's Symposium is also a great day for me, the first time that I have had the pleasure of attending as Dean, and one of my early opportunities to meet the greater Law School community. I see many old, some newer, friends here today, and I am thankful that the Symposium brings us together again. It gives me the chance to make more friends, and I hope and trust that I will be getting better acquainted with many of you in the months and years ahead. The Symposium and I are more or less contemporaries at Columbia. I came here a few years before the Symposium did. The origins of the latter--I am not going to tell you about the origins of the former--can be found in the School's Centennial Conference of 1958. It was an intellectual gathering so successful and so warmly received that the Columbia faculty and alumni decided to repeat it annually.

The late Monrad Paulsen, one of the original organizers, recalled the event. He said: "Apart from the valuable survey of American legal institutions and their prospects, made through the scholarly contributions of the participants, the conference itself was a delightful occasion; several hundred alumni and friends of the School were in attendance." Then as now, three sessions were held. Then as now, there was a luncheon in the Rotunda of Low Memorial Library. Then, but not now, there were groundbreaking ceremonies for a new Law School building. Then as now, there were illustrious moderators. Then, Judge Harold Medina, Walter Gellhorn, and Adolf A. Berle, Jr.; now Vivian Berger, Jack Greenberg, and Arthur Murphy. My thanks to all three. Then as now, the panelists were a distinguished group. Today, as you know, our panelists include nationally and internationally acclaimed human rights advocates, corporate attorneys, public officials, and members of this and other faculties, all of whose names you will find in the program. To all I convey warm thanks. The organizers of the 1958 Centennial Conference no doubt did a fine job, but it is very difficult to imagine their matching the performance of the coordinators of today's event: cochairpersons Judge Uviller and Professor Werner to whom we are all indebted for jobs superbly well done. Thank-you.

Now, it is my particular pleasure and privilege to express on behalf of all here very special thanks to the guiding spirit of this Symposium and of so many other successful alumni events over the last two years: the outgoing president of the Columbia Law School Alumni Association, the Honorable Felice Shea. I have only recently come to know Felice Shea, but, as you know, it doesn't need very long acquaintance with her to have one's admiration and respect, and indeed affection, commanded. I had, of course, heard so many good things about her from mutual friends and colleagues, of her days as a brilliant and dedicated attorney to the Legal Aid Society, of her outstanding reputation on the Civil Court of the City of New York, and now on the Supreme Court of the State of New York. Justice Shea served as first vice-president and director of the Alumni Association, prior to being elected as president in 1984. She is a past Alumni Chairperson of the School's Moot Court Committee and served on the Committee for the Annual Symposium for several years. As president, she has stressed the importance of closer ties between alumni and students, thus helping to strengthen the future of the Association and the School. She has invited representatives of all student organizations to Alumni Association Board of Directors' Meetings so that the students could explain their current needs and, in turn, come to appreciate the role played by alumni in the life of the school. I am delighted to be able to make the first public announcement that Felice Shea will be one of ten distinguished alumni of various Columbia schools to be honored by the Alumni Federation of Columbia University, at the Commencement Day luncheon on May 14th, with this year's Alumni Medal for Conspicuous Alumni Service.

And lest her own school fall short in its recognition and gratitude for her dynamic leadership over the past two years, and all that she has done for the Association in the past, I have been empowered by the membership of the Alumni Association to hand her this small token of our appreciation and affection. While I am at it, I will hand her the podium as well.

JUDGE SHEA: I am going to take a minute to open this present for which I thank all of you very much, even before I see it. It is a very beautiful clock. It is inscribed, and I want to thank each and every one of you for this very beautiful gift. I first want to thank Dean Black for her introduction, but also each one of you for the honor of serving as your president for these past two years. It has been a very great satisfaction to work closely with this great Law School during a period of growth, excellence, vigor, and leadership in the academic community. And as always, you, the alumni, have been and are one of the school's important assets. You share credit and you should take pride in the School's unparalleled accomplishments.

My main role today is to present the Medal of Excellence to a distinguished alumnus, Judge Benjamin Kaplan. In awarding our Medal of Excellence to him, we pay tribute to a man, who after becoming one of the most widely-admired law teachers of his day, went on to a second calling of great distinction as an Associate Justice of the Supreme Judicial Court of Massachusetts. In both those pursuits, as in his earlier work in law practice and government service, he devoted himself to attaining excellence; and far more than most of us, he reached his goal. His career reflects the man and every facet sparkles with quality. On his graduation from Columbia Law School in 1933, he went into practice in New York City with Greenbaum, Wolff and Ernst. He was a member of that firm when World War II broke out, and from it he went into military service. At the war's end, he joined Justice Robert H. Jackson's staff at the Nuremberg trials, and then he returned briefly to his law firm. In 1947, Benjamin Kaplan arrived at Harvard Law School as a visiting professor--and what a visit that was. He stayed for twenty-five years. In 1948 he became a tenured member of the faculty and, in 1961, Royall Professor of Law. The generation of students he taught in the years 1947 to 1972 experienced the thrill of learning law from a teacher who loved what he was teaching, did it superbly, and had the human qualities to inspire, reach, and uplift those he taught.

His aim, as he put it, was to get students to exceed themselves and, from every account, they did. His mastery of the teaching art comes from a unique amalgam of intellect, urbanity, culture, humor, and wit, spiced with a gentle skepticism, and powered by a virtuoso feel for language. He captivated and inspired his students by blending his superb talents with infectious enthusiasm. His mastery of nuance is legendary and between his "quite so" and his "not quite" lay a world of difference. He made memorable use of irony, hyperbole, and farce. One day during the time of the Korean hostilities when a student in his Civil Procedure class answered lamely, he said with a twinkle: "We're talking here about important things. We're not talking about Korea. We're talking about special assumpsit!" Just as Kaplan has brought his perfectionist standard to every task he has undertaken, his unwillingness to fall below that standard may explain why he never in his life has driven an automobile. He has had nevertheless a full agenda.

From 1960 to 1966 he served as reporter to the Advisory Committee on Rules of Civil Procedure of the Judicial Conference of the United States. Under his guidance, the Committee formulated the most substantial revision ever made in those important rules. From 1970 to 1973 he served as coreporter of the American Law Institute's Restatement, Second, of the Law of Judgments. Along the way he coauthored two highly regarded course books; one on copyright and the other on civil procedure. In 1967 he wrote his important treatise, *An Unhurried View of Copyright,* and he told me that he took that title from a well-known treatise of the day called *An Unhurried View of Pornography.* I don't know how many of you have read that, but I think it's an interesting sidelight. That subject became the theme of his Carpentier Lecture at Columbia in 1966. His contributions to this Law School have included service as vice-president of the Alumni Association from 1980 to 1984 and membership on the Law School's Board of Visitors since 1976. Throughout his life, Benjamin Kaplan has used his superb talents as a lawyer, teacher, and judge with an unswerving commitment to making the law and the profession greater institutions than he found them. Our award to him of the Medal for Excellence places that distinguished symbol on the brow of one who wears it with exemplary fitness and grace.

JUDGE KAPLAN: Oh, absolutely beautiful. And very weighty. Judge Shea, I thank you for this medal, I thank the Alumni Association, and I shall cherish the memory of this medal and this event for a long, long time. I am told that I have exactly eight and a half minutes in which to recall old times. So I will jump immediately on September 1930, if you can believe it, when Judge Hopkins and I and these young men here in the Class of 1933 and others, appeared for the first time in the famous class of contracts, presided over by Karl Nickerson Llewellyn. We perceived within the first week that we had arrived at the school at a time when it was involved in an authentic intellectual revolution that went by the name of Legal Realism. Realism put a question to all conventional thinking about law. It asked, what were the ends and objects of law? How determinate or indeterminate was law? Why did the judges behave in the curious ways that they did? What was the connection between law and social science, law and moral philosophy, and so on far into the night? Llewellyn was the apostle of the new thought, but he was not alone. The entire school was in ferment. The curriculum was being torn apart. Conventional case books were being discarded. And new, strange materials were cascading on the heads and shoulders of students. As Abe Feller once said, this was the time when everything mimeographed was good.

So it was an enormously exciting, almost enervating year. And Karl Llewellyn was it for me, and for many others of our troop. A couple of months ago, in the line of duty, I was obliged to read the official history of the Columbia Law School through the fifties. It was written by Professor Julius Goebel, Jr. To my amazement, I found that he had dealt with Llewellyn in one substantive paragraph in which he called the attention of the reader to the fact that Llewellyn had a bad writing style. I consider that rather skimpy treatment. Goebel, who was otherwise a good historian, was a rather zany fellow. I worked for him during summer vacations, and I heard him say repeatedly that in politics he was a monarchist. And I think he was! One of my coworkers screwed up enough courage to ask him: "If you are a monarchist, who is your candidate for king?" He replied without the slightest hesitation: "Harold S. Vanderbilt, of course." Well, some of you out there are too young to remember Harold S., or Hal, as we fellow polo players used to call him, but he, you know, had defended successfully the America's Cup three times. He was also a coinventor of contract bridge. So you see, in the end, Goebel had something.

Well, of course, the second and third years were not as new; they were not as absorbing as the first year, but some faculty pictures come to me very strongly even today. No doubt others would remember other faculty people. There was Milton Handler, who was opening the field of trade regulation as it had never been seen or studied before. There was Robert Lee Hale, a wonderful, loving, and lovable gentleman, who brought political science and economics and a lot of civilization to his seminar in the law of public utilities--public utilities of all things, where for four solid months we examined the rate base. Then there was Jerome Michael, high-class, elegant, and a good teacher, who in those years was involved in one of the most glorious boondoggles of all time. It was an attempt to restate the rules of the law of evidence in symbolic, that is to say, quasi-mathematical form. The symbols were swiped from Russell & Whitehead's *Principia Mathematica*. Now that was a boondoggle. That was a lark. Totally useless, as it seemed to me, but a wonderful experience. We enjoyed it. Finally, there was Herbert Wechsler.

In his second year of teaching--I thought it was his first, but he corrected me--we had a seminar in a new subject: Federal Jurisdiction. Stupid as we fifteen were in that seminar we recognized that we confronted a master. Of course, that is what he was and is. Now you might think after this recital that the Law School was an abode of bliss, that we could say with Wordsworth, "Bliss was it, in that dawn to be alive, but to be young was very Heaven." Not exactly so.

In the first place, the school was extremely rigorous, it was highly competitive, and it was not conspicuously friendly. I will not say it was unfriendly, but it was not markedly friendly. And a second point: If you poked your head out the window, you saw a raging depression. There were people selling apples in the shadow of the statue of Alma Mater right outside this library. That cast a terrible pall over all the life in this country, and the Law School was not excepted. Joy came on March 4, 1933, when the great man came in--even better was March 6, 1933, when by ukase of FDR every damn bank was shut down that was not already shut, and we knew that a strong hand was there. The country was saved. So, the Class of 1933 dispersed. Some went to the New Deal in Washington; the rest of us to private practice. We discovered to our amazement that we had been very well instructed. We were really good, you know. On occasion, we could tell the senior partner what to do. I mean in a legal way. It was terrific. Yes, we knew that we could do it and the school had done it for us.

The Law School has been with us intimately over the past half century and more. We have tried to recall its injunction that we should analyze dispassionately, but act and judge with compassion. I myself have felt, I am bound to say, in private practice and many years of teaching and judging that somehow the old professors were still looking over my shoulder, and they were grading the papers! It is just as hard to achieve an A now as it was fifty years ago. That fixes our loyalty to the school and our affection for it. The school today is a better place, I think, in many ways. It is certainly a more humane place. It does not cohere to a single legal philosophy or vision; it is eclectic, but it is not the worse for that. Of course, the great event in the history of the institution is the election of Barbara Aronstein Black as dean. It is certainly the most interesting event in the history of the place. As a friend and admirer of Dean Black, I am confident that it will be recalled as one of the best events. When Barbara was elected, the revered *New York Times* wrote that the Law School had been on a roll, and I believe, truly, it has been. It is the wish and the hope and the expectation of us veterans and survivors of the memorable Class of 1933 that the school will go forward on a roll for many, many years to come. I don't know that I've expressed what I really feel, but perhaps I will have the chance another time. So, many thanks again and farewell.

JUDGE SHEA: Your newly elected president, Philip A. Lacovara, is going to present today's second Medal of Excellence. It is my privilege to introduce Phil Lacovara to you. He is a member of Hughes Hubbard and Reed in Washington, D. C., a graduate of the Class of 1966, and the son of a Columbia Law School alumnus. He has had a distinguished public career, most notably as Counsel to the Watergate Special Prosecutor in 1973 to 1974. He has also been an active alumnus, a person with profound community and professional concerns, and, I am told, a devoted father of seven children. I know you join me in congratulating him and that you will give him your warm support.

MR. LACOVARA: Thank you very much for that gracious and overly generous introduction. I was elected only this morning, and I want to thank you all for your vote of confidence. Arthur Kimball told me that he was equipped with enough proxies which he had held back from downstate Illinois so that, if there was a Lyndon LaRouche write-in at the last minute, we would still have the election in hand.

My first responsibility as the new president of the Alumni Association is a very happy one for me. It is to read the citation that accompanies the Law School Alumni Association Medal for Excellence being presented to Judge James D. Hopkins. The citation reads as follows:

> "'We are builders, each of us in our own and minuteway of the corpus of the law, which in turn forms the structure of our culture, holding the hope that we are contributing to the betterment of life.' The author of those words has made them his own article of faith and call to action. His contributions as a builder of the corpus of the law are best known through his twenty-two years of distinguished service as a judge. Yet they extend far beyond his judicial career. This gentle, unassuming man has led a life of extraordinary versatility and has filled it with achievement. He has labored not for acclaim but for community. It is especially gratifying to acknowledge the selfless and distinguished contributions of James D. Hopkins by awarding the Columbia Law School Alumni Association Medal for Excellence. Judge Hopkins was graduated from Columbia College with a Bachelor's Degree in June of 1931. Two years later he was awarded the LL.B. by the Law School. However much he derived from his schooling on Morningside Heights, he

has given back far more to the faculty and students of the Columbia community in friendship, kindness, warmth, wise counsel, and devoted service. We are among the most richly endowed of the legions of Hopkins beneficiaries. For more than thirty years he has been an active working member of the Law School Alumni Association. The climax of this facet of his work came in 1978, when he completed a two-year term as president of the Association, and was awarded the Alumni Federation Medal for Conspicuous Alumni Service. The temptation is strong to speak at length about his human qualities, but as a friend once wrote: 'This is not just a nice man.' In the field of public service he accomplished something no one else has ever done. He occupied successively the top positions in all three branches of the Westchester County government: Chairman of its Legislature; the Board of Supervisors; County Executive; and County Judge. From the latter position he went by appointment to the State Supreme Court, and was then elected to a full term. Before long he was appointed by the governor to the Appellate Division, where he served until his retirement in 1981. A colleague of his commented that had the fortunes of political life been slightly different, Judge Hopkins would have been elevated to the New York Court of Appeals and quite possibly to the United States Supreme Court. If that had happened, the colleague continued, 'his outstanding ability, known to us who have worked with him, would have been nationally recognized. He would be hailed throughout America today as one of the nation's great jurists. With us, that is his reputation.' Despite the burdens of work on one of the busiest appellate courts in the land, he has somehow found the time to read widely and to use what he has read. He is cultured and highly intelligent. He has more than high intelligence and even more than deep intelligence. He has perspective, insight, integrity, and generosity. A few years ago when Pace University College of Law needed a dean on an urgent basis, he unselfishly came out of retirement to help them. Besides all that, he is a fine poet, novelist, horticulturalist, and painter. You would not hear any of this from Jim Hopkins. He has such a colossal modesty that praise aimed in his direction simply bounces off. He has demonstrated that a great human being can be a superb public servant."

It is gratifying indeed to be able to recognize these virtues in James D. Hopkins by awarding him the Medal for Excellence.

JUDGE HOPKINS: Yes, you can assist me. I need assistance. Assistance of counsel.

MR. LACOVARA: I hope it's effective assistance of counsel.

JUDGE HOPKINS: It is. This is beautiful. Thank-you very much. Philip Lacovara is justifiably known as a master of advocacy, and it is sometimes said of advocates that they are able to convert black into white--or at least into a neutral gray. I thought as I listened to him just now that he made the subject matter so convincing that even the subject began to believe in what was said, though in my heart of hearts I must tell you that I entertain a reasonable doubt. I recall that on such an occasion as this, Henry James is reputed to have said that he was singularly accessible to demonstrations of regard, and I suspect that all of us are more or less.

Having reached three quarters of a century in age, I claim the privileges that attach to such an advanced state--nostalgia for the past and a stubborn and inalterable belief in the virtues and superior qualities of our Law School in the thirties. The case is proved in my book by simply reciting the names of the faculty in those days: Julius Goebel, whose acerbic wit masked his natural kindness; Karl Llewellyn, whose classroom was alive and stimulating, and, incidentally, whose examinations were noted for their fiendish complexity; Edwin Patterson, who influenced the introduction of new doctrines in contracts and insurance; Adolf Berle, who changed the perception of the modern corporation; Elliot Cheatham, a man of the gentlest sensibilities, who was the first to discern the need for closer emphasis on the role of ethical conduct in an increasingly intricate world; Professor Powell, whose grasp of property law was unparalleled; Milton Handler, Herbert Wechsler, and Walter Gellhorn, who were just beginning their careers and would soon become leaders in their fields; Jerome Michael and Harold Medina and Roswell Magill and Albert Jacobs. I risk the omission of others by faulty memory. These men are unforgettable and have had an indelible effect on my life.

The Class of 1933 entered the Law School just fifty-five years ago, and perhaps I speak with a natural chauvinism in favor of its distinction when I say that to me the year of our graduation marked a watershed in American law. Our class was Januslike. It looked back to an era of essentially private law and looked forward to the new era of the steady emergence of public law. But despite the great changes in almost every aspect of the law, the faculty at the Law School had prepared us to meet the changes and for many of us to take part in the making of the changes. I well remember Dean Gifford telling us after the bank holiday in March 1933, that even though the face of our institutions might be so transformed that lawyers would no longer be needed, men and women of our training would always be needed--just under a different title. Well, lawyers as such survived, but it would be incorrect to say that their roles and judges' roles have not changed in the fifty-odd years since 1933.

I have an incalculable debt to Columbia which I can only acknowledge and never pay. To be honored by you today adds to my debt. I thank you and wish that I commanded the means to make my appreciation as clear as your generosity. I am doubly honored to stand here in the presence of Ben Kaplan, whose brilliant career as scholar and teacher and judge so richly deserves the commendation which you have accorded him. Thank-you all.

JUDGE UVILLER: Ladies and gentlemen, that concludes our program. I hope you will all join us to hear Abe Sofaer shortly. Thank-you.

TERRORISM AND THE LAW

Thirteenth Sulzbacher Memorial Lecture

HON. ABRAHAM D. SOFAER

Introduction by Dean Barbara Aronstein Black

DEAN BLACK: Welcome to the thirteenth Sulzbacher Memorial Lecture. The Sulzbacher lecture series came into being through the generosity of the late Hellen Sulzbacher Krulewitch and her husband, General Melvin Krulewitch, member of the Class of 1918 at the Law School. The lectures honor the memory of Hellen Krulewitch's parents, Isidor and Seville Sulzbacher. Hellen and Melvin Krulewitch were among the School's most loyal friends and most generous benefactors. For many years through the Kruelwitch fellowships, they supported graduate study by students committed to careers in government service or legal education. In 1970, the Columbia Law Library was enriched by receipt of General Krulewitch's rare book collection, comprising sixty-six volumes of sixteenth and seventeenth-century imprints of Coke on Littleton. I know, I needn't remind all you veterans of the Development of Legal Institutions of the significance of Coke's commentary on Littleton's work on land tenures. No doubt you even remember how to spell Coke. But for those in the audience who may not have had the benefit of legal history at Columbia, I will simply say that this is one of the most important works in the literature of the common law, and Columbia now possesses thanks to the Krulewitches, certainly one of the most extensive collections extant of early editions of Coke on Littleton.

In 1984 on the death of Hellen Sulzbacher Krulewitch, Columbia received a substantial bequest, indeed the largest in the school's history, making possible the establishment of the Isidor and Seville Sulzbacher professorship and supporting the continuation of this lecture series. General Krulewitch was also exceptionally generous with his time and organizational talents. He served as director of the Alumni Association, chairman of the Class of 1918, and it was on his initiative that the Association established the Stone-Agers Committee, a group of our senior alumni. The Krulewitches were wonderful friends to the Law School, and I only regret that I returned to Columbia too late to get to know firsthand, as my predecessors were fortunate enough to have done, that they were wonderful people as well.

The list of people that have addressed us as Sulzbacher lecturers includes the Nobel laureate economist Paul Samuelson, constitutional scholar Paul Freund, Elwyn Jones, Lord of Appeal and former Lord Chancellor of Great Britain, historian William E. Leuchtenburg, and the renowned biographer and chronicler of the New Deal era, Joseph P. Lash. Today we are especially fortunate to have with us, as the 1986 Sulzbacher lecturer, a man who very nearly combines in one person the credentials of all those I have just mentioned: teacher, scholar, judge, public servant, lawyer, historian. I don't think he has won the Nobel Prize yet. Abraham D. Sofaer, today Legal Advisor to the U.S. State Department, is better known hereabouts as friend and colleague. Born in Bombay, India, our speaker made his way through the U.S. Air Force, Yeshiva University, N.Y.U. School of Law, where he served as editor in chief of the Law Review, a clerkship with Judge J. Skelly Wright of the U.S. Court of Appeals, and another with Associate Justice William J. Brennan of the Supreme Court. From 1969 through 1979, Abe was a distinguished member of the Columbia Law Faculty, superb teacher, and scholar of great note. His book, *War, Foreign Affairs and Constitutional Power: The Origins,* was hailed by critics and scholars as a fine work of legal history.

In 1979, he was appointed by President Carter to the Federal District Court in Manhattan, where he served with distinction until his current appointment. It is my privilege to present to you the thirteenth Sulzbacher lecturer, the Honorable Abraham D. Sofaer.

TERRORISM AND THE LAW

Terrorism poses important political and diplomatic challenges. It is designed to call attention, through the use of violence, to the causes espoused by terrorists, and to bring about changes in policy favorable to those causes. The United States and its allies--and all other affected nations--must deal with this threat to civilized order with all appropriate measures, ranging from diplomatic to military.

One potential means for dealing with terrorism is law. Americans are particularly attracted to the law as a means for repressing violence, and are committed domestically and internationally to using law to control criminal conduct and to resolve disputes. They invoke the law almost instinctively, and repeatedly, assuming that it regulates international conduct and, in particular, provides a system for bringing terrorists to justice.

Recent terrorist incidents have led to many efforts to use the law, virtually all of which have failed. The law has a poor record in dealing with international terrorism. Some terrorists are killed or captured during the course of their crimes, but few of those who evade these consequences are afterward found and arrested. The terrorist who is prosecuted is likely to be released far earlier than his sentence should require, often in exchange for hostages taken in a subsequent terrorist episode. The time has come to ask, frankly and honestly, why international terrorism is so loudly condemned, and yet so prevalent. What good is the law in fighting international terrorism? Why has it failed?

II

One reason for the law's ineffectiveness is that terrorism, in essence, is criminal activity. In applying law domestically, governments seek to punish and deter crime as effectively as possible. But they recognize that law cannot eliminate crime. They can expect even less of the law in dealing with international terrorism. The world has no international police force or judicial system.

The stock response to complaints about the law's failure to deal effectively with terrorism is that *more* laws are needed. That is a misleading answer. Important gaps do exist in the legal structure that governs terrorist acts, and the Reagan administration is working with Congress and with other nations to close them. For example, the U.S. government lacks a domestic legal basis to prosecute the terrorists who killed an American citizen, Leon Klinghoffer, during the October 1985 *Achille Lauro* cruise ship hijacking, or the terrorists who killed four American civilians on a hijacked Trans-World Airlines flight earlier that year. The Senate has passed a statute establishing jurisdiction for terrorist murders of Americans, and its adoption by the House would be welcome. Americans must not deceive themselves, however, that new laws, closing gaps, will overcome the problems that render law ineffective. Recent events have demonstrated that, even when laws clearly govern particular conduct, they are often disregarded or otherwise fail to achieve their purpose.

The reasons for the law's failure tolerably to control terrorism go much deeper than the absence of law enforcement authority or mechanisms. International law and cooperation in less controversial areas have often proved reasonably effective. In the area of terrorism, however, the law has failed to punish and deter those who use violence to advance their political goals.

Civilized nations have tried to control international terrorism by condemning it, by treating it as piracy, by prosecuting terrorists under the laws of affected states, by creating international norms establishing as criminal certain acts wherever committed, and by cooperating through extradition and other devices in aiding nations attacked by terrorists. An appraisal of these efforts leads to a painful conclusion: the law applicable to terrorism is not merely flawed, it is perverse. The rules and declarations seemingly designed to curb terrorism have regularly included provisions that demonstrate the absence of international agreement on the propriety of regulating terrorist activity. On some issues, the law leaves political violence unregulated. On other issues the law is ambivalent, providing a basis for conflicting arguments as to its purpose. At its worse the law has in important ways actually served to legitimize international terror, and to protect terrorists from punishment as criminals. These deficiencies are not the product of negligence or mistake. They are intentional.

III

Americans too readily assume that others agree that at least certain aspects of international terror are unacceptable. While many fanatics obviously approve of terror, less recognized and more significant is the fact that the acceptance of terror is far more widespread. Indeed, many nations regard terrorism as a legitimate means of warfare.

The United Nations General Assembly began devoting special attention to the subject of terrorism after two especially heinous actions. On May 30, 1972, Japanese terrorists, working with the Popular Front for the Liberation of

Palestine attacked civilian passengers at Lod Airport in Israel with automatic weapons, killing twenty-eight and wounding seventy-eight. On September 5, 1972, terrorists from the Black September organization murdered eleven members of the Israeli Olympic Team in Munich.

On September 8, 1972, U.N. Secretary-General Kurt Waldheim asked for inclusion in the General Assembly agenda of an item entitled "Measures to prevent terrorism and other forms of violence which endanger or take innocent human lives or jeopardize fundamental freedoms." He urged "that all concerned turn away from senseless and destructive violence," and noted that the world community should continue "to exert its utmost influence in seeking peaceful ways" to find solutions "for the problems underlying such acts of terrorism."

The secretary-general's statement evoked angry opposition, which took the immediate form of protests against considering terrorism without considering its causes. The secretary-general reiterated his request on September 20, but acceded to the pressures by adding that it was no good considering terrorism "without at the same time considering the underlying situations which give rise to terrorism and violence in many parts of the world." He assured the protesters that he did not intend "to affect principles enunciated by the General Assembly regarding colonial and dependent peoples seeking independence and liberation."

The two concessions made by Mr. Waldheim may at first glance seem innocuous. In the United Nations, however, they were significant. Attributing acts of terrorism to injustice and frustration obviously tends to excuse, if not justify, those acts. This is especially so when the causes are all assumed to be sympathetic. The language concerning efforts to seek "independence" and "liberation" also implied justification for terrorist acts. These concepts related to the principles adopted in previous U.N. resolutions supporting "self-determination" and wars of national liberation, in the pursuit of which oppressed people were authorized to resort to all available means, including armed struggle.

A General Committee debate on Waldheim's proposal took up the question of terrorism, as well as the concepts of self-determination and wars of national liberation. Many nations opposed adding terrorism to the agenda and strongly suggested their support for certain terrorist actions. For example, the representative from Mauritania said that the expression "terrorist" can "hardly be held to apply to persons who were denied the most elementary human rights, dignity, freedom, and independence, and whose countries objected to foreign occupation." Citing situations in Africa, the Middle East and Asia, he said "such peoples could not be blamed for committing desperate acts which in themselves were reprehensible; rather, the real culprits were those who were responsible for causing such desperation."

In the General Assembly the item was amended to include Waldheim's language on the causes of terrorism and the matter was referred to the U.N. Sixth Committee, on legal affairs. There the representative from Guinea, among others, very clearly supported the right of national liberation movements "to undertake any type of action to ensure that their countries attained independence." The Cuban representative rejected any proposal of "rules for the purpose of assigning legal limits" to revolutionary armed struggle. "The methods of combat used by national liberation movements could not be declared illegal while the policy of terror unleashed against certain peoples was declared legitimate." The Madagascar representative could not have been clearer:

Acts of terrorism inspired by base motives of personal gain were to be condemned. Acts of political terrorism, on the other hand, undertaken to vindicate hallowed rights recognized by the United Nations, were praiseworthy. It was, of course, regrettable that certain acts in the latter category affected innocent persons.

And the Algerian representative presented the philosophical rationale used since time immemorial to justify terror:

His delegation did not agree with the statement in the Secretariat's report that the legitimacy of a cause did not in itself justify recourse to certain forms of violence; those serving the cause in question should have a choice of the means to be used.

These assertions have been repeated in one form or another in the years since that first debate. During this period, the General Assembly passed seven resolutions on terrorism and its causes. The first, adopted on December 18, 1972, had little to say about the type of terrorism which had led to the subject's being placed on the agenda. It expressed "deep concern" over increased acts of violence that took innocent lives or jeopardized fundamental freedoms, and invited states to consider joining relevant conventions. But the resolution was a victory for those who supported the right to use all available measures to advance the ends of self-determination and wars of national liberation. The resolution in fact condemned only one thing: "the continuation of repressive and terrorist acts by colonial, racist, and alien regimes."

A resolution on terrorism adopted in 1977 added another important element. It invited the Ad Hoc Committee on International Terrorism to study *first* the underlying causes of terror, and then to recommend measures to deal with acts of terrorism. A 1979 resolution for the first time condemned acts of terror, but it referred to the 1977 Protocols to the Geneva Convention, which seek to give groups fighting wars of national liberation the protection of the laws of war. Finally, in December 1985, after a further series of terrorist acts, the General Assembly adopted a resolution that "unequivocally condemns, as criminal, all acts, methods, and practices of terrorism." This resolution contains several provisions calling for international cooperation against terrorism. At the same time, however, it reaffirmed each people's inalienable right to self-determination, and the legitimacy of struggles against colonial and racist regimes and other forms of alien domination. The debates preceding and following the adoption of this resolution make clear that many states continue to believe that "wars of national liberation" justify or excuse terrorist acts. For example, the Angolan representative, echoing the comments of the delegates from Algeria, Bulgaria, Kuwait, and Sri Lanka, among others, made it clear that "acts of terrorism could not be equated, under any pretext, with the acts of those who were fighting colonial and racist oppression and for their freedom and independence."

The wide acceptance of the premise that terrorist acts can be lawful in the pursuit of proper goals is an uneasy first lesson. The United States of course also recognizes that oppressed people are sometimes justified in resorting to force, but only if properly exercised. For example, such uses of force must be consistent with the laws of war and should not be directed at innocent civilians, include hostage-taking, or involve torture. In contrast, the U.N. debates and resolutions relating to terrorism do not suggest principled limits on the use of force, or any reasoned, fair-minded basis for determining which peoples are entitled to wage wars of national liberation. The result is a clear signal to all that those groups deemed by the majority to be oppressed will be free legally to use force, and therefore cannot fairly be called terrorists. In other words, acts of terrorism by such groups are not wrong, and the law has no proper role in punishing or deterring such acts.

IV

The legitimacy of political violence is a notion that has also worked its way deep into international law enforcement. Most countries have treaties that obligate them to extradite to other states persons accused of committing, in those states, the crimes associated with terrorism, such as murder, hijacking, bombing, armed assault, and robbery. Yet extradition requests are frequently refused, often because the offense is characterized as "political" conduct which the law exempts from extradition.

Some relatively recent decisions, denying extradition on the ground that the charge is a "political offense," illustrate how detrimental the law can be in the battle against terrorism. In 1972 five individuals hijacked a plane in the United States, extorted $1 million and flew to Algeria, where they were received as political militants. In 1976 they made their way to France, which refused to extradite the five, although they had presented no evidence of political motivation beyond the claim that they were escaping racial segregation in America and were associated with the "black liberation movement." More recently, the United States failed to obtain the extradition of Abu Abbas, thought to have masterminded the *Achille Lauro* hijacking, from two countries through which he passed following the incident (Italy and Yugoslavia). Despite U.S. assertions of their treaty obligation to hold Abbas, these states released him, Yugoslavia claiming that he was entitled to diplomatic immunity because he carried an Iraqi passport. Some decisions byU.S. courts are equally disturbing. In 1959 a federal court refused to extradite Andrija Artukovic to Yugoslavia for the alleged malicious murders of 200,000 Croatians in concentration camps, after determining that these murders were "political." Some twenty-seven years later the United States successfully deported Artukovic, and he is currently standing trial in Yugoslavia. In recent cases U.S. courts have refused to extradite four alleged Irish Republican Army gunmen on the ground that an uprising exists in Northern Ireland, which makes crimes in furtherance of the revolt "political."

How did the United States get to the point of giving sanctuary to terrorists who kill people in order to get their way in a democracy such as the United Kingdom? Or to an alleged mass murderer? The story is both interesting and instructive.

The "political offense" claim as a defense against extradition has noble roots. It developed in the period of the French and American Revolutions, and reflected the value the new democracies placed upon political freedom. Thomas Jefferson commented, for example, that "unsuccessful strugglers against tyranny have been the chief martyrs of treason laws in all countries." At that time political offenses were associated with acts against the security of a state, such as treason, espionage, and sedition.

The concept was soon expanded, however, to so-called relative political offenses--ordinary crimes committed in a political context or with political motivation. An important early case on this point is *In re Castioni*, decided in 1891, in which the English courts denied extradition for a killing that occurred in the midst of a demonstration against the government of a Swiss canton that refused to submit its new constitution to a popular vote. The shooting served no purpose. But the court found it "political" because it was incidental to and a part of a political disturbance. Even if an act is "cruel and against all reason," the court held, its perpetrator is protected if he acted "for the purpose of furthering and in furtherance of a political rising." *Castioni* was quickly qualified in England, when in 1894 one of the many anarchists of the period, Theodule Meunier, was extradited to France for placing bombs in a Parisian cafe and an army barracks. But it took hold in the United States and elsewhere.

In 1894, the same year *In re Meunier* was decided, a U.S. court refused to extradite high officials of El Salvador accused of murders in their unsuccessful effort to retain power *(In re Ezeta)*. Relying on *Castioni*, the court held that all acts associated with an uprising were political offenses. The court accepted without discussion the premise that the doctrine was politically neutral, and that protection should be given equally to democrats and dictators. It also explicitly rejected the notion that the offender's conduct in killing noncombatants could disqualify him from the doctrine's protection. During hostilities, said the court, "crimes may have been committed by the contending forces of the most atrocious and inhuman character, and still the perpetrators of such crimes escape punishment as fugitives beyond the reach of extradition."

The ruling in *Ezeta* had some support in U.S. and foreign practice during the nineteenth century. Granting asylum to revolutionaries and victims of revolutions was seen as enlightened. That was the period during which republican government first became a widespread reality. But the political-offense doctrine has another side. Several incidents, diplomatic decisions and rulings during the nineteenth and twentieth centuries indicate that the United States and other countries have taken their particular interests and political ideals into account in formulating the doctrine's contours. This has led to certain limitations of the concept of a political offense.

A particularly dramatic instance followed the assassination of Abraham Lincoln. Despite the political nature of the crime, the United States sought and obtained assurances from Great Britain and Italy respectively for the apprehension abroad of John Wilkes Booth and John H. Surratt, one of Booth's suspected conspirators. Surratt was actually captured in Egypt and sent back to the United States on an American navy vessel. The need to protect heads of state was recognized by other nations as well, and is now a widely accepted qualification to the political-offense doctrine.

During the American Civil War the United States seized in Morocco, with the acquiescence of the Moorish governor, two Confederate sailors who had gone ashore to obtain coal. An objection was raised that the sailors should have been allowed to assert the political-offense doctrine. Secretary of State William Henry Seward rejected the argument, reasoning that the men were "taken in the very act of war against this government." Similarly, in 1946 France and Belgium agreed to surrender to each other individuals convicted of war-related crimes committed during World War II. One offender sought to defeat a Belgian extradition request by claiming that the spying and assassination with which he was charged were political offenses. The French courts rejected the argument because France could not be deemed a neutral on the issue: "the offense was committed in time of war both against an ally and against France, whose interests were linked."

The more recent problem of aircraft hijacking demonstrates how the doctrine can still be applied in accordance with U.S. national interests. During the 1950s, despite America's strong opposition to aircraft hijackings, the United States and its Western allies refused requests from Czechoslovakia, the U.S.S.R., Poland, Yugoslavia, and other communist regimes for the return of persons who hijacked planes, trains, and ships to escape. But when aircraft hijacking reached epidemic proportions in the late 1960s and early 1970s the United States determined that hijacking of aircraft carrying passengers was too serious a problem and too great a threat to the safety of innocent passengers to be tolerated. The United States reexamined its policy and "concluded that the hijacker of a commercial aircraft carrying passengers for hire should be returned regardless of any claim he was fleeing political persecution."

Thus, the United States suggested in 1969, during consideration of the Hague Convention on Hijacking, that the political-offense exception should be eliminated for that crime. The suggestion was rejected and the political-offense exception was retained, however in both the Hague hijacking convention and the Montreal sabotage convention. Nations therefore remain authorized (though not required) to refuse, on political grounds, to extradite suspects in such universally recognized crimes as hijacking and sabotage.

For several years the United States has been prepared to revise its treaties with democratic allies to narrow the political-offense exception and make it inapplicable to crimes of violence and breaches of antiterrorist conventions. In 1983, for example, the United States signed a revised treaty with Italy that narrowed the political-offense exception to exclude, in certain circumstances, offenses covered by a multilateral agreement, such as the hostage-taking or aircraft hijacking conventions. The United States and its people are opposed to rebellions, revolutions, and political assassination in democracies, since their political systems offer a peaceful means to seek change. Thus, revolutionaries should not be encouraged in a democracy by the treatment of their violent acts as acceptable political conduct. A doctrine born to reflect the United States' belief in freedom should not be permitted to serve the interests of those seeking to impose undemocratic views through force.

To advance this objective, the Reagan administration recently signed a Supplemental Extradition Treaty with the United Kingdom, which narrows the political-offense doctrine to exclude most violent crimes. Similar treaties with other nations are being renegotiated. But the proposed treaty with Great Britain has run into fierce opposition in the Senate. Intense lobbying and strong, emotional concern about the Irish problem may lead the Senate to refuse to ratify this treaty. That would be a grave setback. It would make the United States no better than the other nations that have their favorite terrorists. If the United States fails to reject absolutely the use of force against a democracy that is its closest ally, it will lose credibility in urging other states to cooperate in its own efforts against terrorism.

V

The law against piracy provides another illustration of how international law has failed inadequately to control politically motivated crimes. The *Achille Lauro* incident presented the question whether the acts of the hijackers of that vessel constituted piracy "under the law of nations," and were therefore felonies under U.S. law. The hijackers stole money and jewelry from the ship's passengers, but their primary purposes were political. They were allegedly seeking to commit acts of violence in Israel, where the vessel was scheduled to dock, and after taking control they demanded that Israel release certain terrorists it had imprisoned. Is such an enterprise "piracy"?

The traditional law of piracy could have been one vehicle for obtaining jurisdiction over terrorists, with fewer loopholes for political crimes than recent conventions. Piracy law has long been inapplicable to state vessels and recognized belligerents when they engaged in lawful acts of war. Those who believed that belligerents should not be treated as pirates reasoned that they were the enemies only of a particular government, not of mankind. This recognized exclusion contained a crucial limitation: it applied only if the insurgents confined themselves to depredations against the country with which they were at war. Where individuals engaged in an insurgency attacked nonbelligerents, the exclusion did not apply and the rebels were treated as pirates.

The modern law of piracy purports to modify significantly these traditional rules. The 1982 U.N. Convention on the Law of the Sea and the 1958 Geneva Convention on the High Seas define piracy as any illegal act of violence, detention, or depredation committed against a ship "for private ends." The private-ends requirement was used deliberately to exclude acts with public or political motives. The rapporteur for the International Law Commission, which drafted the Geneva high seas convention, explained that "he had defined as piracy acts of violence or depredation committed for private ends, thus leaving outside the scope of the definition *all wrongful acts perpetrated for a political purpose.*"

The approach of these two conventions would substantially contract the reach of the law of piracy. The "private ends" requirement, at least as described by the rapporteur, would expand the traditional "insurgency" exclusion to cover all persons claiming to be politically motivated. Moreover, the exclusion's traditional limitation to acts committed against a country with which the insurgents are at war appears to have been either overlooked or abandoned. As a result, the conventions arguably place all politically motivated acts outside the universal jurisdiction of sovereign states.

Conceivably, the conventions could be read to cover indiscriminate attacks on civilians, or attacks motivated by race or nationality, having no ordinary relationship to an insurgency, such as the murder of Mr. Klinghoffer. But the terrorists involved in the *Achille Lauro* affair would no doubt claim they were acting politically, even in killing Klinghoffer, and hence could not be called pirates under the conventions.

The "private-ends" requirement undermines some positive achievements contained in the two conventions. The piracy provisions in the conventions were intended to confirm the existence of universal jurisdiction for any nation to capture and punish all persons who committed wrongful acts on the high seas or in the air, or in any other place where no state has jurisdiction. In fact, the conventions go further than merely permitting countries to act. Both contain an article providing that "all States shall cooperate to the fullest possible extent in the repression of piracy" and the commentary to the Geneva Convention on the High Seas states that "any State having an opportunity of taking measures against piracy, and neglecting to do so, would be failing in a duty laid upon it by international law." But by narrowing the definition of piracy, these conventions exclude from the international duty to repress piracy "to the fullest possible extent" all politically motivated attacks on vessels and aircraft.

VI

The exclusion of terrorist acts from the reach of legal prohibitions is not the only means by which law has been employed to legitimize terrorism. Another approach has been to secure for terrorism a legal status that obscures or denies its fundamentally criminal nature. The laws of war mark the line between what is criminal and what is an act of combat. A person who kills someone is normally guilty of homicide. If he does it during combat, however, he is a soldier and can only be held as a prisoner of war, and may be punished only if the killing violates the laws of war. Radical groups responsible for terrorist acts have long sought legitimacy by securing recognition as combatants under the laws of war.

The effort of radical groups to acquire legal legitimacy had a significant success in the Geneva Diplomatic Conference on the Reaffirmation of International Humanitarian Law Applicable in Armed Conflict, which met between 1974 and 1977. The conference, under the auspices of the International Committee for the Red Cross (ICRC), was called to improve the laws of war set forth in the Geneva conventions of 1949. It produced two additional protocols to the Geneva conventions: Protocol I dealing with international, and Protocol II with noninternational, armed conflict. The United States participated in the Geneva conference and signed the protocols, but the President has decided not to seek Senate ratification of Protocol I, and has decided to seek several reservations and understandings as conditions to the ratification of Protocol II.

The ICRC and the conference developed many constructive ideas to help minimize the suffering of combatants and noncombatants in armed conflict. But from the beginning of the conference, an effort was made to extend the law of international armed conflicts to cover activities of the Palestine Liberation Organization (PLO) and other radical groups, many of whom were accorded observer status.

The first substantive address, by then-President Moktar Ould Daddah of Mauritania, urged the conference to recognize "certain values and elementary rights which went beyond the Universal Declaration of Human Rights," because millions were "still under colonial oppression in the African continent, while international Zionism had placed the Palestinian population in an impossible situation." He asked the conference to consider, not only effects, but causes as well, and to recognize "there were such things as just wars." Daddah said, "It was quite obvious that it was the Zionists who wanted to throw the Arabs into the sea....National liberation movements did not want to shed blood, only to secure recognition of their rights."

The Geneva diplomatic conference adopted in its first session what is now Article 1(4) of Protocol I, with 11 of 99 nations, including the United States, abstaining, and only Israel dissenting. This article would make the laws of international armed conflict applicable to "armed conflicts in which peoples are fighting against colonial domination and alien occupation and against racist regimes in the exercise of the right of self-determination." Never before has the applicability of the laws of war been made to turn on the purported aims of a conflict. Moreover, this provision obliterated the traditional distinction between international and noninternational armed conflict. Any group within a national boundary claiming to be fighting against colonial domination, alien occupation, or a racist regime can now argue that it is protected by the laws of war, and that its members are entitled to prisoner-of-war status for their otherwise criminal acts. Members of radical groups in the United States have already tried to do so in federal courts.

The 1CRC and most Western nations expressed no admiration for this article. Some contend, however, that as a result of the new rule humanitarian law now governs the actions of national liberation groups. While the PLO and other "freedom fighters" may now claim the benefits of the laws of war, they thereby became bound to obey these rules. This, in some eyes, is seen as an advance for humanitarian law.

In fact, radical groups rarely have the resources and facilities to provide the protections for prisoners of war required by the laws of war. Even if they had the resources, these groups have no inclination to provide such protections, or to abide by the law's limitations on the actions they may take, particularly against noncombatants. In fact, the supporters of Article 1(4), no doubt recognizing that the PLO and some other "freedom fighters" have concentrated their guns, bombs, and rockets on civilian noncombatants, obtained an additional protection for these groups. Article 44(1) provides that, once a group qualifies as a national liberation movement, protected by Article 1(4), no conduct by individual members of the group can lead to the loss of its status as a protected organization. The rationale for this rule is that individuals should be punished separately for their conduct. The effect is to preserve the right of such organizations to be treated as combatants, even if they routinely engage in acts of terror against civilians.

The Geneva diplomatic conference went even further in accommodating the needs of radical groups, at the expense of the civilian population that humanitarian law is intended to protect. A fundamental premise of the Geneva conventions is that, to earn the right to protection as military fighters, soldiers must distinguish themselves from civilians by wearing uniforms and carrying their weapons openly. Thus, under the 1949 Geneva Convention on Prisoners of War, irregular forces achieve combatant (and, if captured, prisoner-of-war) status when they (1) are commanded by a person responsible for subordinates, (2) bear a fixed, distinctive insignia recognizable from a distance, (3) carry weapons openly, and (4) conduct their operations in accordance with the laws and customs of war. Fighters who attempt to take advantage of civilians by hiding among them in civilian dress, with their weapons out of view, lose their claim to be treated as soldiers. The law thus attempts to encourage fighters to avoid placing civilians in unconscionable jeopardy.

The terrorist groups that attended the conference had no intention of modifying their conduct to satisfy these traditional rules of engagement. Terrorists are not soldiers. They don't wear uniforms. They hide among civilians and, after striking, they try to escape once again into civilian groups. Instead of modifying their conduct, therefore, the terrorist groups succeeded in modifying the law.

Article 44(3) of Protocol I recognizes that "to promote the protection of the civilian populations from the effects of hostilities, combatants are obliged to distinguish themselves from the civilian population while they are engaged in an attack or in a military operation preparatory to an attack." But the provision goes on to state "that there are situations in armed conflicts where, owing to the nature of the hostilities, an armed combatant cannot so distinguish himself." In such situations, "he shall retain his status as a combatant, provided...he carries his arms openly: (a) during each military engagement, and (b) during such time as he is visible to the adversary while he is engaged in a military deployment preceding the launching of an attack in which he is to participate." Furthermore, the section provides that "acts which comply with the requirements of this paragraph shall not be considered as perfidious"--for example, feigning protected status prior to a military engagement by using signs, emblems, or uniforms of the United Nations, or nations that are not parties to the conflict.

These changes in traditional rules undermine the notion that the protocol has secured an advantage for humanitarian law by granting revolutionary groups protection as combatants. Under the Geneva conventions, a terrorist could not hide among civilians until just before an attack. Under Protocol I, he may do so; he need only carry his arms openly while he is visibly engaged in a deployment or while he is in an actual engagement.

These changes have more than merely symbolic significance. The radical groups represented at the conference lobbied hard for them and succeeded. After the vote on Protocol I, the PLO's representative "expressed his deep satisfaction at the result of the vote, by which the international community had reconfirmed the legitimacy of the struggles of peoples exercising their right to self-determination." He then specifically cited Article 1(4) as authority for the PLO's actions in Israel.

VII

Protocol I's recognition of wars of national liberation recently received rhetorical and symbolic reinforcement in what one would have thought was a mostly unlikely place: the U.N. Convention Against the Taking of Hostages. The convention, adopted by the General Assembly in 1979, makes criminal the taking of hostages, requires nations to enact implementing legislation, and imposes an extradite-or-prosecute obligation. Nearly thirty countries, including the United States, are currently parties to the convention. One extraordinary provision *precludes* extradition where the suspect is likely to be unfairly treated, thus providing a ready excuse for refusing to extradite. But the obligation to prosecute remains. On the whole, the convention establishes a useful scheme for combating hostage-taking by terrorists, a goal that the U.N. Security Council reaffirmed on December 18, 1985, by the adoption of a resolution condemning unequivocally all acts of hostage-taking and abduction.

A review of the negotiating history of the Convention Against the Taking of Hostages, however, reveals the deep division over the propriety of terrorist acts. The negotiations began in 1977 and were completed in 1979. At the outset, a number of countries sought to exclude from the convention hostage-taking by national liberation movements. Some states, including Libya, went further and sought not only to exempt such movements, but to define hostage-taking to include the act of subjecting persons to colonialism, racism, or foreign domination. In other words, all the people living in a country determined to have a racist government would be deemed to be hostages, and the government to be a hostage-taker.

These radical proposals were eventually rejected during the 1979 session. Advocates of political violence did, however, win a significant victory. The nations that opposed excluding liberation movements from the coverage of the convention were required to accept a reference, in Protocol I to the 1949 Geneva conventions, to the treatment of national liberation fighters as combatants. This reaffirmation took the form of Article 12 of the hostage-taking convention, which provided that, to the extent the 1949 Geneva conventions and the 1977 additional protocols impose substantively identical obligations with regard to an instance of hostage-taking, the hostage-taking convention will not apply to the armed conflicts ("in which peoples are fighting against colonial domination and alien occupation and against racist regimes in the exercise of the right of self-determination") specified in Article 1(4) of Protocol I.

Article 12 of the hostage-taking convention does not, in my view, create a legal gap in coverage. All instances of hostage-taking remain subject to an obligation by the state in which a hostage-taker is found either to extradite or to prosecute. Nevertheless, the states that sought this provision succeeded in using the hostage-taking convention to achieve a rhetorical and political victory. They can now argue that the structure and language of Article 12 represent some measure of acceptance that members of national liberation movements are combatants, not terrorists, since hostage-taking by such movements are covered by the laws of war and excluded from the convention. The delegate from Yugoslavia, for instance, expressed the view that the committee considering the convention had, by its action, "reaffirmed...that the struggle of the liberation movements was legal, that it was based on provisions of international law of war and that it could not be confused with the criminal activity of irresponsible persons and terrorist groups and organizations."

It is comically bizarre to suggest, as Article 12 requires in specified circumstances, that persons like Abu Abbas must be treated as wayward soldiers, rather than as international criminals. That the laws of war and the laws against hostage-taking have been structured to permit that result reflects the strength of influence terrorist organizations and their supporters now wield in international law.

VIII

Not all diplomatic efforts to quell terrorism have been as negative as the foregoing. For example, the 1973 Convention on the Prevention and Punishment of Crimes Against Internationally Protected Persons, Including Diplomatic Agents, is generally considered a successful negotiation by the West. It is interesting, however, to examine the manner in which certain countries, after failing to change the text of this convention, managed nonetheless to obtain concessions that serve their purpose of circumventing its clear and absolute obligations.

In 1973 the U.N. General Assembly adopted the protected persons convention, and over sixty nations are currently parties, including the United States. The convention defines a class of internationally protected persons, and requires governments to make criminal certain violent acts directed against such persons or their property, and to extradite or prosecute suspected offenders found in their territory. The convention text is nonpolemical, and its coverage is relatively comprehensive--not surprising when one realizes that it was drafted, negotiated, and adopted by its principal beneficiaries: diplomats.

What is surprising, however, is how close the negotiations came to being derailed, and the lack of underlying consensus that the discussions reflect.

The Sixth Committee of the United Nations began considering the draft version of the protected persons convention on October 4, 1973. On November 15, when agreement had been reached on the majority of the provisions, the delegate from Mali, on behalf of a group of thirty-six countries, introduced a proposed additional article that caught many other delegations by surprise. The article would have made the protected persons convention inapplicable to "peoples struggling against colonialism, alien domination, foreign occupation, racial discrimination, and apartheid in the exercise of their legitimate rights to self-determination and independence." The Mali delegate, stating a theme repeated by others, claimed the article was needed to prevent the convention from "serving as a pretext for colonial and racist regimes to intensify the suppression of the national liberation movements recognized in various United Nations decisions and resolutions." The delegate from Morocco said his delegation could not favor a convention that would protect the governmental agents of certain states "against all risks." The brutal truth is that, by implication, the proposed article advocates that the right of self-determination include the right to commit violent acts against diplomats.

This position was unacceptable to the United States as well as others. It was eventually rejected after intensive behind-the-scenes negotiations between November 15 and December 6, but on a basis that cast a pall over the exercise. The United States acquiesced in a Sixth Committee recommendations to the General Assembly that it adopt, along with the draft convention, a resolution recognizing that nothing in the protected persons convention could "in any way prejudice the exercise of the legitimate right to self-determination and independence...by peoples struggling against colonization, alien domination, foreign occupation, racial discrimination, and apartheid." In addition, Paragraph 6 of the resolution declared "that the present resolution, whose provisions are related to the amended Convention, shall always be published together with it." While these provisions cannot be considered law, they are a clear indication of what many governments believe, and of the muscle those states were able to bring to bear in getting the resolution adopted as part of a package deal.

This put the United States on notice that, in the future, other governments may rely on the resolution to circumvent the absolute obligations of the protected persons convention itself. In fact, Burundi's accession to the convention reserved the right not to apply its terms to national liberation movements, and Iraq indicated when it acceded that it intended to accord protected status to the representatives of certain national liberation movements. In short, even so seemingly neutral an issue as the protection of diplomats failed to escape the political divisiveness that pervades the world community on questions of the appropriate use of violence.

IX

The law's support for political violence has been manifested most recently in the efforts of some nations to establish doctrinal bases for curtailing the use of force against terrorists and their supporting states.

International law regulates the use of force by a country in the territories of other states, whether to capture or attack terrorists or to rescue hostages located there, or against the states themselves for sponsoring terrorists or conspiring with them in specific terrorist activities. In general, a nation may *not* enter upon another territory without its consent. Similarly, a state may not stop, board, divert, or otherwise interfere with another's vessels or aircraft without some adequate basis. Finally, the use of force against another country's territorial integrity or political independence is prohibited, except in self-defense, and any use of force must be both necessary and proportionate to the threat it addresses.

These principles have been respected by the United States. If they were applied however in such a manner as to preclude any use of force for any purpose, international law would serve to insulate the perpetrators of international violence from any control or punishment for their crimes. States could then continue using terrorism to accomplish their objectives with little cost or interference.

The principle of territorial sovereignty is not the only principle of law that must be weighed in considering objections against attacks on terrorists, attempts to rescue hostages, and actions against countries that sponsor terrorism. States have duties to cooperate in preventing terrorists from using their territories in perpetrating criminal acts, and many governments have explicitly undertaken to extradite or prosecute terrorists guilty of hijacking, sabotage, and hostage-taking. These obligations cannot be disregarded in evaluating the propriety of antiterrorist operations. Furthermore, under the U.N. Charter, just as under customary international law, victims of terrorism are not powerless to defend themselves. The charter reaffirms the *inherent* right to use force in individual or collective self-defense against armed attack.

Since the days of President James Madison, the United States has repeatedly acted against armed bands that attacked Americans and then fled, seeking sanctuary in neighboring countries unwilling or powerless to prevent or punish their acts. With the acquiescence of the harboring state, as in the case of U.S. operations in Mexico against Pancho Villa's terrorist attacks in the early part of this century, or without such permission, as in the case of Andrew Jackson's actions to stop attacks from Spanish Florida, the United States has used its forces to bring an end to terrorist attacks on American citizens and interests.

Other nations, when confronted with terrorist attacks, have defended themselves with force. In the celebrated case of the *Caroline*, the British pushed over Niagara Falls a ship carrying some members of an armed band of New Yorkers that was in the process of supporting an insurrection in Canada. While the American government thought the British had acted too harshly, both governments agreed on the law: the use of force in self-defense is appropriate so long as it is

Court of Justice recognized the principle in the *Corfu Channel* case, where Britain had swept mines from the channel after suffering damage to its ships. In holding Albania liable for the damages, the court reaffirmed the "well-recognized" principle that every country has an obligation "not to allow knowingly its territory to be used for acts contrary to the rights of other States."

As Secretary of State George Shultz has said, in the fight against terrorism as in the struggle to deter aggression:

The law is a weapon on our side and it is up to us to use it to its maximum extent....[A] state which supports terrorist or subversive attacks against another state, or which supports or encourages terrorist planning and other activities within its own territory, is responsible for such attacks. Such conduct can amount to an ongoing armed aggression against the other state under international law.

Some public officials and international law experts have questioned the premise that harboring and supporting terrorists who attack a nation is a form of aggression. Others suggest that force may not be used against a government that sponsors terrorist acts. The United States has never accepted such a paralyzing view of the right to act in self-defense. Strong legal support exists for the U.S. position on these issues, as reflected in universally recognized principles of conspiracy and agency law and in several U.N. resolutions, including the Friendly Relations Declaration and the U.N. Definition of Aggression. Here, as in other areas, states and individuals opposed to U.S. policies, or to the use of force in general, are invoking law as a mask for their political interests.

The U.S. bombing raid launched against Libya on April 14, 1986, illustrated the need nations sometimes have to use force against states that sponsor terrorism. After terrorists from the Abu Nidal group attacked passengers in Rome and Vienna on December 27, 1985, killing nineteen civilians, including five Americans, President Reagan clearly signaled the United States' intent to rely upon its right of self-defense. He said:

By providing material support to terrorist groups which attack U.S. citizens, Libya has engaged in armed aggression against the United States under established principles of international law, just as if he [Libyan leader Muammar al-Qaddafi] had used its own armed forces.

Despite this clear warning, Libya deliberately arranged for at least two attacks aimed at American noncombatants and U.S. interests. One plan was to fire automatic rifles and hurl grenades at civilians lined up at the U.S. embassy in Paris. French cooperation enabled the United States to thwart this plan, and several Libyans involved were deported. The United States was not so fortunate in West Berlin. Libyans at their people's bureau (embassy) in East Germany informed their home base that a planned attack would take place on April 5. A bomb exploded at a discotheque frequented by U.S. soldiers, killing Sergeant Kenneth T. Ford and a Turkish woman, and injuring over 200 persons, including 50 Americans. Shortly thereafter, on April 6, the same people's bureau informed Tripoli of the successful attack, and assured Tripoli that the bombing could not be traced to Libya.

These communications, following Qaddafi's long history of support for terrorism, and his threats against U.S. citizens, established overwhelmingly that Libya was responsible for the attack. In addition, the President was faced with strong evidence of some thirty possible impending Libyan attacks on U.S. facilities and personnel throughout the world. The April 14 strikes were to deter these and other planned attacks.

Some governments have condemned the action against Libya, claiming to disbelieve U.S. claims that Libya attacked American citizens and was planning further attacks. Others have ignored U.S. claims, and simply characterize Reagan administration actions as "criminal" or "brutal." They oppose the use of force, even in self-defense. But no cogent argument has been made questioning the legal principles upon which the United States has relied. A resolution condemning the United States was vetoed by the United States, France, and the United Kingdom in the Security Council on April 21. Its adoption would have given state-sponsored terrorism its ultimate legal defense, immunizing international aggression against noncombatants from the use of force in self-defense.

Law can make clear that state-supported terrorism is illicit, and may thus serve to deter it. But terrorist-supporting nations will not surrender seriously held ambitions to expand their power and influence simply because the law is against them. Legal argument alone will not protect law-abiding nations and peoples against Qaddafi or Iran's Khomeini. Nor will the prospect for peaceful settlement of disputes with such regimes be enhanced by U.S. promises to abjure force or by unrealistic limits on its flexibility. If Americans overestimate the limits of their own tolerance, they may allow U.S. adversaries to do so as well, thereby inviting reckless activity. The policeman is apt protection against individual criminals; but national self-defense is the only protection against the criminal state.

X

The law, as presently formulated, cannot reasonably be expected effectively to repress international terrorism. International terrorism is still supported by many nations as a legitimate means of struggle against regimes deemed by them to be colonial, alien, or racist. At the behest of these states, and by the acquiescence of others, international law has been systematically and intentionally fashioned to give special treatment to, or to leave unregulated, those activities that cause and are the source of most acts of international terror.

The failure of international law to control terrorism is a matter of great strategic concern. Ineffective methods for dealing with terrorists through the law will inevitably lead to antiterrorist actions more primitive and dangerous than cooperation among sovereign states, including conventional military actions in self-defense, will provide. These dangers are especially heightened with terrorism that is state-supported.

Civilized nations and peoples cannot give up on law, however frustrated they may feel with its shortcomings. In fact, the point of this essay is that law is not presently being used to counter terrorism; it has been placed very much at the service of those who embrace political violence. Our challenge is to create a broader understanding among peoples and governments to bring about a shift in the objects that international law is designed to serve.

APPENDIX

Twenty-seventh Annual

COLUMBIA LAW SCHOOL SYMPOSIUM 1986

Including the Sulzbacher Memorial Lecture

Saturday, April 5, 1986

Sponsored by

The Columbia Law School Alumni Association

PROGRAM

LAW SCHOOL BUILDING

9:15 a.m. CONTINENTAL BREAKFAST
Ground Floor

9:45 a.m. ANNUAL MEETING OF THE
COLUMBIA LAW SCHOOL ALUMNI
ASSOCIATION, INC.
Room E, Ground Floor

10:00 a.m. MORNING PANEL DISCUSSIONS

1. THE ROLE OF LAW AND LAWYERS
IN SOUTH AFRICA

Moderator:

JACK GREENBERG '48
Professor of Law and Vice-Dean,
School of Law, Columbia University

Panelists:

LOUIS HENKIN
University Professor, Columbia University

SYDNEY KENTRIDGE
Senior Counsel, Johannesburg, South Africa
Attorney for the families of Steve Biko
   and Winnie Mandela

SONNY VENKATRATHNAM
Former Political Prisoner
Member of the Unity Movement
   Durban, South Africa

168 • *Appendix*

2. CAN TORT LAW HANDLE MODERN
   INDUSTRIAL ACCIDENTS?

   Moderator:

   ARTHUR W. MURPHY '48
   Joseph Solomon Professor of Law in Wills,
      Trusts and Estates, Columbia University

   Panelists:

   LUCINDA M. FINLEY '80
   Associate Professor of Law, Yale
      University

   STEPHEN B. MIDDLEBROOK
   Vice-President and General Counsel,
      Aetna Life & Casualty Company

   WILLIAM F. KENNEDY
   Of Counsel, Hunton & Williams

   GENE LOCKS '62
   Partner, Greitzer & Locks

3. NEW LIMITATIONS ON DEFENDANT'S
   RIGHT TO COUNSEL

   Moderator

   VIVIAN O. BERGER '73
   Professor of Law,
      Columbia University

   Panelists:

   RUDOLPH GIULIANI
   U.S. Attorney,
      Southern District of New York

   GARY NAFTALIS '67
   Partner, Kramer, Levin, Nessen,
      Kamin & Frankel

H. RICHARD UVILLER
Professor of Law,
  Columbia University

12:30 p.m. COCKTAIL RECEPTION AND LUNCHEON
           LOW MEMORIAL LIBRARY

Honoring:

HON. JAMES D. HOPKINS '33
Former Justice of the Supreme Court of
  New York, Appellate Division, Second
  Department
Former Westchester County Executive

HON. BENJAMIN KAPLAN '33
Former Justice of the Supreme Judicial
  Court of Massachusetts
Royall Professor of Law, Emeritus
  Harvard University

Judge Hopkins and Judge Kaplan are the
recipients of the Columbia Law School
Alumni Association Medal for Excellence.

Presiding:

HON. RENA K. UVILLER '62
Judge, Court of Claims, State of New York

Welcome:

BARBARA ARONSTEIN BLACK '55
Dean of the Faculty of Law,
George Welwood Murray Professor of Legal
  History, Columbia University

Joseph M. Proskauer Auditorium
Ground Floor, Law School

2:30 p.m. SULZBACHER MEMORIAL LECTURE

TERRORISM AND THE LAW

Speaker:

ABRAHAM D. SOFAER
Legal Adviser,
U.S. State Department

4:00 p.m. STUDENT MUSICAL

THE BEST LITTLE LAW SCHOOL IN HARLEM

SCHOOL OF INTERNATIONAL AND
PUBLIC AFFAIRS
Altschul Auditorium, Ground Floor

Following the performance there will be an alumni-student cocktail reception in honor of the cast. George Bowen Case Lounge, 7th Floor, Law School

THE COLUMBIA LAW
SYMPOSIUM COMMITTEE

RENA K. UVILLER '62, Alumni Chair

WALTER WERNER, Faculty Chair

COMMITTEE

Richard T. Andrias '70
Edward Ross Aranow '32
Clarence S. Barasch '35
Bernard Baumrin '70
Richard J. Bauerfeld '35
Dean G. Braslow '61
Bertram Braufman J'48
Joseph Calderon '39
Austin Campriello '71
Vicente Ang Casim '67 MCL
Leonard N. Cohen J'49
Barbara Ann Cook '71
Nanette Dembitz '37
Meyer Eisenberg '58
Carol R. Farhi J'47
Lucinda M. Finley '80
Edith L. Fisch F'48
Mary E. Freeman '76
Nicholas G. Garaufis '74
James P. Gerkis '83
Jason R. Gettinger '67
Mary A. Giannapoulou '58 MCL
Keith O. Goffney '83
Susan I. Grant '77
Don David Grubman '79
Allen Harris '54
Robert M. Heller '66
M. David Henkle '31
Robert F. Herrmann '73
Lauren B. Homer '77
Elizabeth Hornstein '69
Fred Taylor Isquith '71

Monroe I. Katcher, II '31
Alvin H. Kaufer '43
Arthur O. Kimball
Darryl J. Kramer '73
Donna Krone '75
Christoph Kuhmann '84 LL.M.
David M. Levitan J'48
Anne S. Lombard '83
Andrew M. McBride, III '75
Howard N. Meyer '36
Barbara C. Molinsky '53
B. Anthony Morosco '61
Andres Ochoa-Bunsow '80 LL.M.
Ira J. Palestin '24
Clyde E. Rankin, III '75
Raymond Reisler '29
C. Paul Rogers, III '77 LL.M.
Robert R. Salman '64
Kim Leslie Shafer '84
Stephen C. Sherrill '78
Edith I. Spivack '32
Robert L. Tofel '57
Robert B. Viner '81 LL.M.
Arthur Wachtel '28
Constance Z. Wagner '80
Evelyn E. West '32
Stephen M. Wiseman '84
Nancy Young '79

COLUMBIA LAW SCHOOL
ALUMNI ASSOCIATION 1985-86

OFFICERS

Felice K. Shea, President
Philip A. Lacovara, First Vice-President
Edward J. Barshak, Vice-President
Ernest Bonyhadi, Vice-President
Theodore I. Botter, Vice-President
Alfred J. Boulos, Vice-President
David A. Braun, Vice-President
H. F. Lenfest, Vice-President
William S. Singer, Vice-President
Neil A. Smith, Vice-President
Virginia G. Watkin, Vice-President
C. Christopher Alberti, Secretary
Willys H. Schneider, Treasurer

BOARD OF DIRECTORS

Joseph Calderon
Albert J. Cardinali
Arthur A. Feder
Robert M. Heller
Kay C. Murray
Clyde E. Rankin, III
Felice K. Shea
Susan P. Thomases

Murray J. Laulicht
Mary B. Lehman
Ira H. Lustgarten
Arthur Markewich
Harriet F. Pilpel
William B. Pollard, III
Ruth G. Schapiro
Abraham Tannenbaum

Victor M. Earle, III
Esteban A. Ferrer, III
Carl E. Kaplan
Alfreida B. Kenny

Robert P. Knapp, Jr.
Philip A. Lacovara
Constance B. Motley
Myra Schubin

Clarence S. Barasch
Franklin Feldman
John S. Martin
Horace Michelson
Michael Ellmore Patterson
Judith A. Reed
Judith P. Vladeck
Kathleen A. Warwick

STUDENT DIRECTORS

Stephen A. Overton
Monica D. Medina

BOARD OF ADVISORS

Harold R. Medina
A. Donald MacKinnon
Charles D. Breitel
Lawrence E. Walsh
Edward Ross Aranow
Stephen P. Duggan
Milton Pollack
Harold L. Russell
Wilfred Feinberg

James D. Hopkins
William W. Golub
Eugene H. Nickerson
Stanley L. Temko
William C. Warren
Michael I. Sovern
Albert J. Rosenthal
Benno C. Schmidt, Jr.
Barbara Aronstein Black

Arthur O. Kimball, Executive Director
Stephanie Straffi, Alumni Relations Officer